1981

William I. Kaufman's

Pocket Encyclopedia of California Wine

PUBLISHED BY
THE WINE APPRECIATION GUILD
SAN FRANCISCO

Published by The Wine Appreciation Guild
1377 Ninth Avenue
San Francisco, Ca 94122
(415) 566-3532
957-1377

ISBN 0-932664-11-1

Library of Congress Catalog Card Number 80-51654

Printed in The United States of America

Cover Design: Bill Lansberg
Typography: Vera Allen Composition
Editors: Ken Hoop
            Maurice Sullivan

Contents

Foreword

In 1858, Col Agoston Haraszthy predicted: "It is beyond
a doubt that California will produce as noble a wine as
any part of Europe; when it will have the proper varieties of grapes and the most favored localities in soil
and climate are discovered."

One hundred and twenty-two years later those localities have certainly been discovered in what has become
known around the world as the California Wine Country. It is also certain, as Col. Haraszthy had predicted,
that California produces as noble a wine as any part of
Europe.

This wine encyclopedia provides the clues to one of
California's most enjoyable treasure hunts. The search
through our wine Country is almost as rewarding as
the tasting of our wines. This erudite but quite readable
little volume will help any reader develop an appreciation for California wines and enhance an appreciation
already acquired.

March Fong Eu
California Secretary of State

Introduction

The Pocket Encyclopedia of California Wines is a "first"
in many ways. It is the "first" pocket encyclopedia ever
published on the subject of California wines. It is the
"first" California wine book published in a small easy
pocket size. It is the "first" totally objective book on the
subject of California wine in that I have not imposed
my "favorites" on you the reader. It is a reference book
with suggestions and a broad list on the subject of
varietal wines that you might want to try. I do not tell
you what is best. When it comes to telling you what is
best, I have not backed off from making a decision. I
simply made the decision that the results of the Orange
County Fair 1980 Commercial Wine Judging Awards
were the most important recommendations that I could
make to you. Judging was done on a blind basis, no
labels showing, no pre-conceived judgements could be
made. Wines were not submitted for judging. A total of
733 wines were purchased from retail stores and were
divided into 11 varieties and 39 classifications. The
judges were representatives of 36 California wineries.
This is what I call the best of judging and that is why
I have stepped back to let the judges (many who are
winemakers) make specific suggestions through the
award system.

The other important factors of this book are that it
will give you an easy reference guide to all of the wineries and vineyards in California and help explain some
of the terminology that is associated with wine. There
is always the possibility that I have omitted a winery.
If I have done this and you want to bring it to my
attention, please do so. Please keep in mind that this
is a pocket size book and I have tried to give you a
treasury of information that will help enrich your wine
life and at the same time provide you with an easy
reference source.

I have told you what my pocket encyclopedia is and
now I would like to tell you what it *is not*. This *is not*
a visitors guide to the wineries of California. For that
reason I have not included any information pertaining

to the subject of visiting and tasting. It *is not* a vintage guide to the best wines and their years. I have purposely left out the inclusion of vintage years with each wine and have indicated whether or not wineries vintage date their wine. However, we have included a brief chart of the vintages by district, as there have been some truly outstanding years. My reason for this is simple. All California wines are not available all over the United States since the majority of wineries are small or medium size. Telling someone that the 1968 Chateau Jacqueline from Napa was one of the greatest and then that person not being able to go out and purchase it is one of the most frustrating experiences to the wine lover.

On the other hand, I have done my best to tell you something about the winery (providing there was something to say or the winery was willing to share information with me). I tell you about the wines that are produced, vintage dated, estate bottled and the secondary label if there is one.

On the matter of definitions; I have included those definitions that will cover the broad range of wine drinkers from the serious winophile to the "not too serious but enjoys a good glass of wine" drinker.

Never before in the history of wine books has there been a vintage date on the cover. As life changes everyday, so does the California wine business. It is the desire of the publisher and myself to add new wineries, new wines and the results of important tastings to each new year's pocket encyclopedia. Thus the reason for our vintage dated book. For the price of one medium priced wine your pocket encyclopedia will open the door to several thousand bottles of wine depending on your pocketbook and interest. Most importantly the *Pocket Encyclopedia of California Wine* will help expand your knowledge of the world's most exciting wine region. I have learned from creating this book and I am certain that the same shall be true with you.

I want to thank all of the wineries and the California Wine Institute for their help and encouragement. A special thanks to Ms. J. Simon for her constant faith in the book and invaluable help.

William I. Kaufman

A

ACACIA WINERY

2636 Las Amigas Road, Napa, CA 94558

Napa County

Storage: French Oak

The winery is a limited partnership. The general partners are Gerry Goldstein and Michael Richmond. The winemaker is Larry Brooks. Founded in 1979. The vineyards are located in the Carneros region and is 50 acres of Chardonnay. Pinot Noir is purchased from select vineyards. Also Chardonnay.

100% varietal, vintage dated, Estate Bottled Chardonnay is produced. Also produced are 100% varietal, vintage dated St. Clair Vineyard Pinot Noir, Lee Vineyard Pinot Noir, Iund Vineyard Pinot Noir, Winery Lake Chardonnay, Napa Valley Chardonnay and Tempesquet-Santa Barbara Chardonnay. The winemaker's favorite is St. Clair Pinot Noir.

Acidity

In wine, acidity is the word normally used to indicate the quality of tartness to the taste; i.e. to the presence of agreeable fruit acids, an important favorable element in wine quality. Not to be confused with "sour" or dryness or astringency.

Acids

Natural acidity in grapes (and new wines) is mostly tartaric and malic acids; after Malo-lactic "secondary" fermentation, the malic acid has changed into softer tasting lactic acid, but the tartaric acid remains unchanged through it all. Tartaric, in fact, remains unchanged through long-term bottle aging as well. (Tannins soften with age, but acids don't change unless the wine is chilled enough to cause cream of tarter to crystallize out of solution.) When that happens, you can see crystals on the cork or in the bottle but, even then, the taste of the wine is not usually changed significantly. Acidity gives the wine its "tart" taste, but equally important, acidity helps to protect the wine from spoilage, during fermentation and during aging later.

ADOBE CELLARS NEGOCIANTTS

5789 Dexter Circle, Rohnert Park, CA 94928

Negociant offers varietal wines in the $3.99 range. Current offering in Cabernet Sauvignon.

Ageing

Wine develops smoothness, mellowness and character in ageing. Everything that happens to wine during ageing is not yet fully understood by scientists. However, many things are known: the grape solids are deposited, the wine clarifies itself, some oxidation occurs as the wine "breaths" through the wood casks and the many complex natural elements of the wine slowly interact or "marry" for smoothness. Other complex natural changes also occur. These changes are the most mysterious. They create in the wine elements of flavor and bouquet, substances called aromatic esters and other compounds that are not found in grapes, grape juice or new wine.

Age is not a positive guide to quality. Most of the world's wines complete their ageing quite early, even losing quality with further storage. Ageing usually begins in large tanks holding from 5000 to 200,000 gallons each. Some wineries prefer wood, others concrete tanks lined with special coating and others use glass-lined steel or stainless steel tanks. As wines mature many producers complete the ageing in smaller wood containers. Oak is favored by some, but redwood is also much in use. Casks of 1,000 gallons, oval shaped to make the lees deposit in a small space at the bottom, are preferred by many. Some finish the ageing in even smaller casks or barrels. The smaller the container of wood, the greater the ratio of surface through which the wine can "breathe" and take on the flavor characteristics of the container.

AHERN WINERY

715 Arroyo Ave., San Fernando, CA 91405

Los Angeles County

Storage: 60 gallon barrels

Owners are James and Joyce Ahern. Winemaker is James P. Ahern

Varietal, vintage-dated wines produced are Zinfandel, Sauvignon Blanc and Chardonnay.

AHLGREN VINEYARD

20320 Hwy 9, Box 931, Boulder Creek, CA 95006

Santa Cruz County

Storage: French and American oak barrels

The owners are Dexter and Valerie Ahlgren. The winemaker is Dexter Ahlgren. Vineyard is located on the San Lorenzo watershed, in the Santa Cruz mountains. Grapes are also purchased on a select vineyard basis. Founded in 1976 and won the top Gold Medal for their '77 Cabernet Sauvignon in the 1979 Los Angeles County wine judging.

Varietal, vintage dated wines produced are Monterey County Chardonnay and San Luis Obispo County Cabernet Sauvignon.

The winemaker's favorite wine is the San Luis Obispo County Cabernet Sauvignon.

ALAMEDA COUNTY
A north central coast county.
Appellations: Livermore, Livermore Valley.
Wines to look for: Richard Carey, Concannon, Montclaire, J.W. Morris, Numano Sake, Oak Barrel, Rosenblum, Stonyridge, Veedercrest, Villa Armando, Weibel, Wente Bros., Wine and the People, Fretter Wine Cellars.

ALAMEDA, CONTRA COSTA

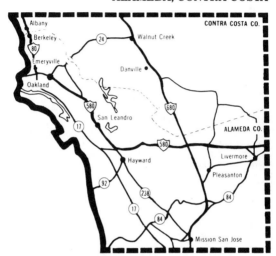

ALATERA VINEYARDS
5225 St. Helena Highway, Napa, CA 94558
Napa County
Storage: Oak cooperage and St. steel
Owners and Winemakers, Bruce M. Newland and Holbrook T. Mitchell. Vineyards are in Napa County. Grapes are supplied by growers who are stockholders.
Varietal vintage dated wines produced are Chardonnay, Cabernet Sauvignon, Gewurztraminer, Late Harvest Bunch Sel. Hust. white Riesling, Pinot Noir and Paradis (white Pinot Noir)

Alcohols
The major alcohol in wine is ethanol. Table wines with low ethanol content have a thin character, and those with too high a concentration often have a "hot" taste. The other alcohols, never present in large concentrations, can be considered flavor components, especially in contributing something to the "nose" of the wine.

Alcohol Content
Average % Alcohol Content of wine: Aperitif, 12% – 31%; Red, white, rosé and champagne, 12% – 14%; Dessert, 17% – 21%

Aleatico
(Sweeter Fortified Wine) A varietal grape occassionally used for sweet table or dessert wine. It is related to the muscats originally imported from Italy.

ALFONSO
(See Bisceglia Bros.)

Alicante Bouschet
A prolific grape rarely used as a red table wine. Predominantly used in Burgundy blends for color. Heavily planted in San Joaquin Valley. Originally came from Spain. Available as a varietal from Papagni Vineyards. Estate Bottled.

ALEXANDER VALLEY VINEYARDS
8644 Hwy 128, Healdsburg, CA 95448
Sonoma County
Storage: 55 gallon oak barrels and st. steel.

The general partner and winemaker is Harry H. Wetzel, III. Purchased acerage in 1963 on original homestead of Cyrus Alexander who homesteaded the land in 1842. Vineyard is located at winery in Alexander Valley.

100% varietal, vintage-dated, Estate Bottled wines produced are Chardonnay, Johannisberg Riesling, Gewurztraminer and Chenin Blanc. Also, Cabernet Sauvignon (80–90%, balance Merlot) Pinot Noir and Zinfandel (1982).

The winemaker's favorite wines are Johannisberg Riesling and Chardonnay.

ALMADEN
1530 Blossom Hill Road, San Jose, CA 95118
Santa Clara, San Benito, Alameda and *Monterey Counties*
Storage: white oak, French oak, Hungarian oak, Redwood, st. steel

The Owner is National Distillers, Inc. Klaus Mathes is the winemaker. The vineyards are spread over four counties that grow 29 grape varieties.

Varietal wines all show appellation-of-origin and vintage. The varietal wines produced are: San Benito Pinot Chardonnay, San Benito Pinot Blanc, Monterey Sauvignon Blanc, Monterey and San Benito Johannisberg Riesling, San Benito Gewurztraminer, San Benito Grey Riesling, Monterey Chenin Blanc and French Colombard, San Benito Pinot Noir, Monterey and San Benito Cabernet Sauvignon, San Benito Gamay Beaujolais, San Luis Obispo Merlot, Petite Sirah, Monterey Gamay, San Benito and Monterey Zinfandel, Ruby Cabernet, Grenache Rose and San Benito Gamay Rosé.

Also produced are: Chablis, Burgundy, Mountain Nectar Vin Rosé, Sweet and Pale-Triple-Dry Vermouth, Flor Fino, Solera, Cocktail, Solera Golden, Solera Cream and Service Ace Sherry. Tinta Ruby and Tinta Tawny Port.

The Almaden "Mountain" wines are Mountain Red Claret, Red Burgundy, Red Chianti, White Chablis, White Sauterne and Rhine.

The sparkling wines are Brut, Extra Dry and Pink Champagnes, Sparkling Burgundy, Eye Of The Partridge, and Chardonnay Nature. Blanc de Blanc carries a cuvee date.

The La Domaine Champagnes are: Brut, Extra Dry and Pink. Also sparkling Burgundy and Select Cold Duck.   *(continued)*

The label bearing the name, Charles LeFranc founder wines are: San Benito Late Golden Johannisberg Riesling, San Benito Chardonnary, Monterey Cabernet Sauvignon, Pinot St. George, Founders Port, Maison Rouge and Maison Blanc.

ALTA VINEYARD CELLAR
1311 Schramsberg Road, Calistoga, CA 94515
Napa County
Owners, Benjamin and Rose Falk; Winemaker, Jon P. Axhelm; Vineyards Napa Valley/North Coast, 10 acres.

Alta was founded in 1878 by Colin T. McEachran. In 1880 Robert Louis Stevenson visited Alta and his visit was described in his chapter on Napa wine in "Silverado Squatters". In 1970 the Falks bought Alta and replanted the vineyard in Charbonnay. Vintage-dated, Estate-bottled Chardonnay is produced.

ALTA VISTA
(See Grand Pacific Vineyards)

AMADOR COUNTY
(Sierra Foothills)

Appellations: Shenandoah Valley, Fiddletown.

Wines to look for: Amador Winery, Argonaut Winery, D'Agostini Winery, Montevina Wines, Kenworthy Vineyards, Stoneridge, Shenandoah Vineyards, Santino Winery.

AMADOR, CALAVERAS, EL DORADO, SACRAMENTO, TUOLUMNE

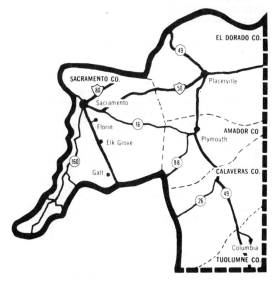

AMADOR WINERY
P.O. Box 166, Amador City, CA 95601
Amador County
Storage: French and Spanish oak   *(continued)*

Owners, Leland F. Merrill and Harry Ahrendt. Winemaker is Harry Ahrendt.

Wines produced are Sutters Gold and Mountain Jubliee.

AMBASSADOR

(See Perelli-Minetti)

Americans for Wine

A nationwide organization to bank together wine consumers interested in the wellbeing of wine in the United States.

Americans For Wine, a voluntary grassroots network, will provide a forum for consumers, growers, restaurants, retailers, wholesalers and wineries as a cohesive, independent group to express a collective view on public policy issues that affect wine. Members receive periodic newsletters and bulletins.

To join send $1 to: Wine Institute (the Trade Association of the California Wine Industry), 165 Post St., San Francisco, CA 94108.

S. S. ANDERSON VINEYARD

1473 Yountville Crossroad, Napa, CA 94558

Napa County

Storage: Small French cooperage, st. steel.

Owners, Stanley and Carol Anderson; Winemaker, Stanley Anderson; Vineyards, 49 acres in Napa Valley.

Varietal, Estate-Bottled wines produced are, Chardonnay, Sparkling Cuvee de Noir and Sparkling Cuvee de Chardonnay.

ANDRÉ

(See E. & J. Gallo)

Angelica

A white dessert wine, traditionally one of the sweetest wine types. It is either straw or amber-colored and mild and fruity. Angelica originated in California and is produced from a number of grape varieties, including Grenache and Mission. Good with or following dessert, and with between-meals refreshments. Serve chilled or at room temperature. Most common sacramental wine. Look for: Assumption Abbey, Novitiate, San Martin, Mt. La Salle, East-Side, J. W. Morris.

Aperitif Wine

French word from the medieval Latin "Aperire," meaning "to open," and refers to wine and other drinks taken before meals to stimulate the appetite. In the strictest sense, it applies to vermouths and other wines flavored with herbs and other aromatic substances, but in general usage, any wine when served before a meal may be referred to as an "aperitif."

Appellation

Term which signifies the geographical origin of a wine. When the appellation of origin appears on the label, 75% of the wine must come from grapes grown in that region.

Appetizer Wines

Wines enjoyed before the meal. Sherry and Vermouth, the main appetizer wines, range from extra dry to sweet in taste.

Appleness
   A frequent characteristic of fine white wine.

ARGONAUT WINERY
   Willow Creek Road, Ione, CA 95640
   Amador County
   Storage: Oak, redwood, st. steel.
   W.M. Bilbo, managing partner. Winemaker is Neal Overboe.
   Founded 1976. Varietal, vintage dated wines produced are Zinfandel and Barbera.

Argols
   The tartrate deposited by wines during aging.

Aroma
   That part of the fragrance of wine which originates from the grapes used, as distinguished from "bouquet."

ARROYO SONOMA
   (Previously Bandierra Wines)
   155 Cherry Creek Road, Cloverdale, CA 95425
   Sonoma County
   Founded 1937. Mark Black and Chris Bilbro, Owners and Winemakers.

ASSUMPTION ABBEY
   (See Brookside)

Astringency
   The quality of causing the mouth to pucker. The degree of astringency of a wine depends primarily upon the amount of tannin it has absorbed from the skins and seeds of the grapes. Moderate astringency is a desireable quality in many red wine types. Not to be confused with dryness. Never call an astringent wine "sour."

Atmosphere
   The unit of measure for pressure of wine in a bottle of sparkling wine or Champagne. Air pressure at sea level is equal to 1 Atmosphere. At 50°F, sparkling wines have 1.5 Atmospheres. It increases to 2.8 Atmospheres at 80°F. This is why the bottles have metal cork retaining wires. Always open away from another individual.

B

Balance
   Denoting complete harmony in the principal constituents of the wine. Excessive amounts of one over another causes disharmony of palate impression and wines so constituted are described as "poorly balanced" or "unbalanced."

BALDINELLI/SHENANDOAH VALLEY VINEYARDS
   Plymouth, CA 95669
   Amador County
   Storage: French and American 50–60 gal. barrels.
   Owners—John Miller and Edward Baldinelli; Winemaker—Edward Baldinelli; Vineyards—70 acres.
   Amador County—Shenandoah Valley
   Varietal, vintage-dated, Estate-bottled wines produced

are: Amador County, White Zinfandel, Zinfandel Rosé and Zinfandel. Also, Cabarnet Sauvignon.

BALI HAI

(See United Vintners)

Balling

The system for measuring soluble solids in grape juice, which are mostly sugars. Balling degrees indicate sugar content. Similar to Brix.

BALLARD CANYON CORPORATION

1825 Ballard Canyon Road, Solvang, CA 93463
Santa Barbara County
Owners—The Hallock Family. Founded 1978.
Varietal, vintage dated wines produced are Santa Ynez Valley-Cabernet Sauvignon, Santa Ynez Valley-Dry Johannisberg Riesling and Santa Ynez Valley-Cabernet Sauvignon Blanc.

BALVERNE WINE CELLARS

P.O. Box 70, 10810 Hillview Road, Windsor, CA 95492
Sonoma County

BANDIERA WINERY

(Now called Arroyo-Sonoma)

Barbera

(Red Table Wine)
A varietal grape. Produces red, full-bodied, dry and tannic wine. Will age up to 10 years. Excellent accompaniment to pasta, sea food and fish stews, when young. Aged Barbera is excellent with game. Originally from the Piedmont district of Italy. Labels to look for: Bargetto, Bynum, Giumarra, Heitz, Louis Martini, Montevina, Papagni, Ridge, Sebastiani.

BARENGO

3125 East Orange Street, Acampo, CA 95220
San Joaquin County
Storage: Oak cooperage, redwood and st. steel.
Founded 1934
The owner is Ira Kirkorian; Winemaker is Mark Caporale.
The Barengo vineyard provides the grapes for their estate-bottled Chenin Blanc and French Colombard along with their generic wines. Grapes for their other varietals are selected from vineyards in the Lodi area and in the Central Coast region.

The varietal wines produced bear a vintage date and vineyard or area appellation. They are Chenin Blanc, French Colombard, Johannisberg Riesling, Chardonnay, Muscat Pantelleira, Zinfandel, Petite Sirah, Cabernet Sauvignon. Generic wines are White Calif. Vintners Reserve Wine, Rose Calif. Vintners Reserve Wine and Red Calif. Vintners Reserve Wine. Dessert wines are Cremapri, Cremocha, Ambermint and Crema Marsala. Barengo also produces the Dudenhoe for May Wine.

BARGETTO WINERY

3535-A North Main Street, Soquel, CA 95073
Santa Cruz County
Storage: Oak, redwood and st. steel.   *(continued)*

Founded 1933

Owner is the Bargetto family; the winemaker is Lawrence Bargetto.

Four other members of the family also work at the winery. Grapes are purchased on a selective district basis. Primary sources are San Luis Obispo and Santa Barbara Counties. Winery has won many medals at tasting competitions.

The varietal, vintage-dated wines are French Colombard, Chardonnay, Zinfandel, Late Harvest Zinfandel, Pinot Noir, Cabernet Sauvignon, and Late Harvest Semillon.

The other varietals are Gamay Rose, Chenin Blanc, Moscato Amabile and Johannisberg Riesling.

Also Chablis, Burgundy, Moscato Scuro, Vin Rosé Dolce, Champagne, Port, Sherry and a selection of fruit and berry wines.

The winemaker's favorites are Chardonnay, Johannisberg Riesling and Cabernet Sauvignon.

Baume

The measure of the sugar content of the grape. One Baume is equal to approximately 1.75% of sugar content.

BEAUJOLAIS

(See Gamay)

BEAULIEU VINEYARD

1960 St. Helena Highway, Rutherford, CA 94573

Napa County

President of Beaulieu is Legh F. Knowles; Winemaker is Thomas B. Selfridge and Dimitri Tchelistcheff is Technical Director. The vineyards are near the winery in central Napa Valley, while grapes for BV Pinot Noir and Pinot Chardonnay are grown in the Carneros region of southern Napa.

The varietal-Estate bottled wines produced are: Cabernet Sauvignon, Pinot Noir, Gamay Beaujolais, Grenache Rosé, Pinot Chardonnay, Johannisberg Riesling, Muscat de Frontignan and Sauvignon Blanc.

Generic wines are: Chablis, Burgundy, Beaurose, Pale Dry and Cream Sherry, Brut Champagne and Champagne de Chardonnay. Whenever conditions warrant it, there is a limited selection known as Georges de Latour Founder's Wines.

JOHN B. BECKETT CELLARS

1055 Atlas Peak Road, Napa, CA 94558

Napa County

Founded 1975

Owner, John Beckett

Varietal, vintage-dated wines produced are Cabernet Sauvignon and Johannisberg Riesling.

BEAU VAL WINES

Star Route #2, Box 8D, 10671 Valley Drive, Plymouth, CA 95669

Amador County

Storage: Small oak cooperage.

Owners—Vernon Gilman, Scott Harvey and Nan and Robert Francis; Winemaker—Vernon Gilman

(continued)

Vineyards in Amador County. Varietal wines produced are Zinfandel, Barbera and Sauvignon Blanc.

BEL ARBRES
(See Fetzer Vineyards)

BELL CANYON
(See Burgess Cellars)

BELLA NAPOLI WINERY
121128 So. Austin Road, Manteca, CA 95336
Founded 1934
Owner, Estate of Tony R. Hat
Vineyard—60 acres; Brands—Vine Flow, Family Vineyard, Ala Sante.

BELLROSE VINEYARD
435 W. Dry Creek Road, Healdsburg, CA 95448
Sonoma County

BERINGER VINEYARDS
2000 Main St., St. Helena, CA 94574
Napa and Sonoma Counties
Storage: Nevers, Limousin, Yugoslavian, and American Oak, Redwood and st. steel.
Founded 1876
The owner is the Nestle Company of Switzerland; Winemaker is Myron S. Nightingale.
The 2,000 acres of vineyards are in the Napa and Sonoma Valleys. Each vineyard has been planted to grow specific grapes. The vineyards are Knights Valley, Gasser, St. Helena, DeCarle, Gamble, Yountville and Big Ranch Road.
The Beringer-labeled varietal wines are Cabernet Sauvignon, Grignolino, Pinot Noir, Zinfandel, Chardonnary, Johannisberg Riesling, Fume Blanc, Chenin Blanc, Grey Rieseling, Gamay Rosé and Gamay Beaujolais.
The Los Hermanos-labeled wines are Chablis, Burgundy, Vin Rose, Rhine, Gamay Beaujolais, Zinfandel, French Colombard, Chenin Blanc and Cabernet Sauvignon.
The Winemaker's favorites are: "Beringer" Cabernet Sauvignon, Chardonnay, Fume Blanc, Johannisberg Riesling, Cabernet Sauvignon Port and "Los Hermanos" Cabernet Sauvignon.

BERKELEY WINE CELLARS
(See Wine and the People)

BERNARDO WINERY
1333 Paseo del Verano Norte, San Diego, CA 92128
San Diego County
Storage: Redwood vats
Founded 1898
The Owner and Winemaker is Ross Rizzo. He is a fifth generation winemaker. Vineyards are in San Diego County.
Wines produced are: Zinfandel, Muscat, Tokay, Carignane and Mission.

BERTERO WINERY
3920 Hecker Pass Highway, Gilroy, CA 95020
Santa Clara County   (continued)

Storage: Redwood tanks, oak casks.

Owner and Winemaker is Angelo C. Bertero.

The vineyard is located near the winery. The original 1906 planted vineyard is still producing Cabernet Sauvignon. 100% varietal, vintage-dated wines produced are: Grignolino, Barbera (North Coast), Cabernet Sauvignon and Grenache Rosé.

Other wines produced are: Burgundy (Grenache, Carignane and Barbera), Chablis (100% French Colombard) and Zinfandel (Santa Clara and Amador Counties). The Winemaker's favorite wines are: Barbera and Grignolino.

BIG SUR
(See Monterey Peninsula Winery)

Big Wine
A tasting term to express body and fullness and apparent fruitiness.

C. BILBRO WINERY
2062 Mill Creek Road, Healdsburg, CA 95448
Sonoma County

Binning
Bottle-aging of newly-bottled wines, usually in bins, before release for sale.

BISCEGLIA BROTHERS WINE CO.
25427 Avenue 13, Madera, CA 93637
Founded 1880.

The President of the winery is Bruno T. Bisceglia. Other label names are: Paradise, Canterbury, Alfonso F. Bisceglia, Old Rosé and La Croix.

Wines produced under the Bisceglia label are: Burgundy, Chablis, Pink Chablis, Rhine, Vin Rosé Chenin Blanc and Cabernet Sauvignon.

Black Muscat
A dessert wine made from one of the Muscat grapes. Sweet and high in alcohol content (12%–20%). A Ruby Port type taste medium to deep red, rich fruity and full-bodied. Produced only by Novitiate. (See Muscatel)

Blanc de Blancs
White wine made from white grapes.

Blanc de Noir
White wine made from black grapes, by fermenting must without the the presence of skins. The excellent Domaine Chandon Champagne is made in this manner, and the label indicates this.

Blending
The art of mixing wines of various qualities and characteristics to make a better quality wine and insure uniformity from year to year.

Body
Consistency, thickness or substance of a wine, as opposed to the lack of body in a thin wine. Body of a wine reflects the quantity of solid matter, or "extract," in solution in the liquid and, more particularly, the alcohol content.

BOEGER WINERY
1709 Carson Road, Placerville, CA 95667   *(continued)*

El Dorado County
Storage: Small oak cooperage and st. steel
Founded 1973
The owners are Gregg and Susan Boeger.
Gregg Boeger is the Winemaker. The vineyard is located at the winery. Grapes are also purchased on a selected *district* basis.
Varietal vintage-dated wines produced are: Chardonnay, Sauvignon Blanc, Chenin Blanc, Johannisberg Riesling, Zinfandel, Cabernet Sauvignon. Also Chablis.
"Hangtown Red", a blended red wine, is also produced.

JACQUES BONET
(See United Vintners)

BOONE'S FARMS
(See E. & J. Gallo)

BORRA'S CELLAR
1301 E. Armstrong Road, Lodi, CA 95240
San Joaquin County
Storage: Oak barrels
Founded 1975
Owners, Stephen and Beverly Borra; Winemaker is Stephen Borra.
Vineyards are located at winery. Wine produced is Barbera.

Botrytis
Called "Pourriture Noble" in France, "edel faule" in Germany, translated means "noble rot." Botrytis cinera when the white grapes become shrunken, pinkish raisins covered with grey mold. If nature infects the grapes with Botrytis at just the right time (after they have matured to around 17° Brix), and if the humidity then alternates between high and low levels, and if it doesn't hail or rain too much, and if the temperature remains warm long enough for the mold to grow and concentrate sweetness in the grape cluster to levels approaching 30 degrees, then it is possibly a great year for a classic dessert wine that once only places like Barsac, Sauterne, Rhine and Mosel were capable of producing. But no longer is this true, California has its own fabulous Botrytis wines.

Bottled in Bond
A term used to indicate bottled under Government supervision on bonded premises.

Bottle Sizes
Half gallon: 64 oz., 1.75 liters, 59.2 oz.
Magnum: 51.2 oz., 1.50 liters, 50.72 oz.
Quart: 32 oz., 1.00 liters, 33.8 oz.
Fifth: 25.6 oz., 750 mil, 25.4 oz.
Pint: 16.0 oz., 500 mil, 16.9 oz.

BOUNTY
(See California Growers Winery)

Bouquet
That part of the fragrance of the wine which originates from fermentation and aging, as distinguished from "aroma", the fragrance of the grape in the wine.

B. & P. WINERY
1611 Spring Hill Road, Petaluma, CA 94952
Sonoma County

B. & R. VINEYARDS, INC.
4350 No. Monterey Highway, Gilroy, CA 95020
Santa Clara County
President and Winemaker—John P. Rapazzini. Brand Names: Rapazzini, Los Altos, San Juan Bautista.

BRECKENRIDGE CELLARS
(See Giumarra Vineyards)

Brix
The system used for measuring the soluble solids in grape juice. A measure of sugar, Brix degrees range from 0° to about 40°.

J.F.J. BRONCO WINERY
6342 Bystrum Road, Ceres, CA 95307
Stanislaus County
Storage: stainless steel.
Founded 1973.
The Owners are John G., Jr., Joseph S. and Fred T. Franzia. The winemaker is John G. Franzia, Jr.
The three dynamic and knowledgeable Franzias grew up in the wine industry at the Franzia Brothers Winery. The three severed ties with the family winery after it was acquired by Coca-Cola Bottling Co. of New York, in 1973. They founded the Bronco Wine Company in 1973. Vineyards are located at the winery.
Wines produced under the J.F.J. label are: Chablis, Ruby Rosé, Rich Burgundy, Pink Chablis, Rhinewine, Chablis Blanc, Sangria, Bambis Blush, Champagne, Pink Champagne and Cold Duck. Wines produced under the C-C Vineyard label are: Chablis, Pink Chablis, Vin Rosé, Burgundy, Champagne, Pink Champagne, and Cold Duck.

BROOKSIDE
9900 Guasti Road, Guasti, CA 91743
San Bernardino County
Storage: Oak, redwood, st. steel
Founded 1832.
The Owner is Beatrice Foods. The Winemaker is Bill Wieland.
·The President of Brookside is René Biane, the grandson of Biane, who started to work at Brookside in the late 1800s, and married the daughter of the founder, Theopile Vache. Brookside is the oldest continuing vineyard in business, having started in 1832. The vineyards are located in the Cucamonga, Temecula and Sonoma districts. Wines produced under the Brookside Celler label are: Chablis, Sauterne, Haute Sauterne, White Chianti, Dry Muscat, Burgundy, Claret, Chianti, Vino Rosso, Vin Rosé, Rosé Soave, Light Sweet Red, White and Muscat. Port, Sherry, Muscatel and Angelica.
Wines produced under the Assumption Abbey label are: Pinot Chardonnay, Johannisberg Riesling, St. Èmilion, French Colombard, Emerald Riesling, Vertdoux Blanc, Chablis, Rhine, Haute Sauterne, Pinot St.

George, Cabernet Sauvignon, Pinot Noir, Petite Sirah, Ruby Cabernet, Zinfandel, Pinot Noir, Burgundy, Gamay Beaujolais, Vin Rosé, Grenache Rosé, Sherry, Port, Marsala, Angelica and Muscat.

Wines produced under the Vaché label are: Cabernet Sauvignon, Petite Sirah, Ruby Cabernet, Chenin Blanc, St. Emilion, Gamay Beaujolais, Riesling, Grenache Rosé, Pinot Chardonnay, Sherry, Madeire, Chablis, Rhine, Vino Bianco, French Colombard, Burgundy, Zinfandel, Barbeone, Pink Chablis, Sherry, Port and Champagne. They operate a chain of wine tasting stores throughout California.

DAVID BRUCE WINERY

21439 Bear Creek Road, Los Gatos, CA 95030
Santa Cruz County
Storage: Oak barrels and st. steel.
The Owner is David Bruce. The Winemaker is Stephen Miller. Vineyard is located at the winery in the Santa Cruz Mountains.
Varietal, vintage-dated wines produced are: Cabernet Sauvignon, Chardonnay, Pinot Noir, White Riesling, Zinfandel, Petite Sirah and Gewurztraminer.
The Winemaker's favorite wine is the Chardonnay.

Brut

The epitome of dryness, usually applied to Champagne, which means that little, or no, "dosage" has been added to the wine.

Brut

Dry Champagne. No sweetness.

BUEHLER VINEYARDS

820 Greenfield Road, St. Helena, CA 94574
Napa County.
Storage: Oak barrels and st. steel
Owner—John P. Buehler Sr.; Winemaker is John Buehler, Jr.; Vineyards—60 acres are in Napa County. Varietal wines produced are Zinfandel, Cabernet Sauvignon and Sauvignon Blanc.

BUENA VISTA WINERY

18000 Old Winery Road, Sonoma, CA 95476
Sonoma County
Founded 1857
Owner—A. Racke of Germany; Winemaker, Don Harrison.
The Winery was founded in 1857 by Agoston Haraszthy who is considered to be the founder of the California Wine Industry. Haraszthy visited the Estate of the former Mexican Governor of the region and purchased several hundred acres, then set out his own vines, bottling the first vintage in 1857. In 1861 he returned to Europe, selecting the choicest varieties, including the Pinot Chardonnay, Pinot Noir, Gewurztraminer and Cabernet Sauvignon. In all, he had over 100,000 cuttings of 300 varieties. He returned to California with the cuttings, not only for Buena Vista, but also, for all wine growers in the State. Buena Vista's Winery is an official histor-

ical landmark. Vineyards are located at the winery and in the Carneros region.

Varietal, vintage-dated wines produced are: Pinot Chardonnay, Johannisberg Riesling, Gewurztraminer, Green Hungarian, Sauvignon Blanc, Cabernet Sauvignon, Zinfandel, Pinot Noir, Gamay Beaujolais and Cabernet Rosé. Those that are Estate-bottled are indicated on the label. Also produced are: Chablis, Burgundy, Sherry and Port. Periodically, special conditions prevail and Buena Vista Cask Wines (Red) and Buena Vista Cabinet wines (White) are produced. Winemaker's favorite wines are: Estate Chardonnay and Estate Cabernet Sauvignon.

Bulk Wines

Wines which are stored, shipped or packaged in containers usually having a capacity of five gallons, or more.

BURGESS CELLARS

1108 Deer Park Road, St. Helena, CA 94574
Napa County
Founded 1880
Owner—Tom Burgess; Winemaker—Bill Sorenson.
The vineyard is located at the winery, which was started by the original homesteaders, about 1880. Varietal, vintage-dated wines produced are: Chardonnay, Cabernet Sauvignon, Zinfandel, and Petite Sirah. Wines have won many awards.

Burgundy

The name used to describe generous, full-bodied, dry red dinner wines, with a pronounced flavor, body, and bouquet and a deep red color. California Burgundy is made from a number of different grape varieties, including Gamay, Petite Sirah, Pinot Noir, Carignane and Zinfandel.

Pinot Noir, Gamay, Petite Sirah, Pinot St. George Burgundy-type wines, named for the grapes from which they are principally made, having the flavors and names of their respective grapes: California wine made from them has a velvety-soft body and a deep, rich bouquet.

BURGIO

(See J. Carey Cellars)

Butt

A wine cask with the capacity of 100 to 140 gallons.

DAVIS BYNUM WINERY

8075 Westside Road, Healdsburg, CA 95448
Sonoma County
Storage: Oak, redwood, st. steel.
Owner and Winemaker is Davis Bynum. Grapes are purchased on a selective basis from vineyards predominantely in Sonoma County. The winery has been the recepient of many medals at various tasting competitions.

The varietal wines produced are: Zinfandel, Pinot Noir, Gamay Beaujolais, Cabernet Sauvignon, Fum;æ Blanc and Pinot Chardonnay. Also, Sonoma Chablis and Sonoma Burgundy.

The Winemaker's favorite is Allen-Hafner Private Reserve Chardonnay.

C

CACHÉ CELLARS

Pedrich Road, Davis, CA 95616

Owners, Charles and Elizabeth Lowe; Winemaker, Charles Lowe.

Cabernet Franc

One of two Cabernet grape varieties. Franc is the leading variety of the St. Emilion District of Bordeaux. Small plantings in the north coastal counties of California. Franc yields a lighter quicker maturing wine than Sauvignon. Excellent in Rosés.

Cabernet Sauvignon

(Red Table Wine). A varietal grape capable of producing prestigious wines. This wine is dry, full-bodied and capable of great complexity if allowed to age. When young, Cabernet Sauvignon has a dominant tannic characteristic. Originally from the Bordeaux region of France where it is one of the principal grapes for the great Chateaux Clarets. The intensive ruby-red color deepens with age. A classic accompanyment with beef, lamb or duck. Also enjoyable with a fruit and cheese: Brie, Port Salut, Cheddar or Roquefort.

Look for: Alexander Valley, Almaden, Beaulieu B.V. Private Reserve, Burgess, David Bruce, Buena Vista, Cassyre-Forni, Caymus, Chappellet, Chateau Chevalier, Clos du Bois, Clos du Val, Concannon Ltd., Cuvaison, CakeBread, Chateau St. Jean, Chateau Montelena, Richard Carey, Diamond Creek, Dehlinger, Dry Creek, Durney, Fetzer, Felton Empire, Freemark Abbey, Firestone, Franciscan, Foppiano, Geyser Peak, Gemello, Giumarra, Gundlach-Bundschu, Heitz, Hoffman Mountain Ranch HMR, Inglenook Cask, Jordan, Kenwood, Keenan, Charles Krug, Matanzas, Mount Eden, Mountain Side, Mayacamas, Mt. Veeder, Robert Mondavi, Montevina, Louis Martini, Oakville, Joseph Phelps, Pedroncelli, Parducci, Raymond, Rutherford Hill, Ridge, Roudon-Smith, Stag's Leap Wine Cellars, Shenandoah, Spring Mountain, Sterling Reserve, Sonoma, Simi, Stonegate, San Martin, Sanford and Benedict, Silver Oaks, Trefethen, Veedercrest, Zaca Mesa, Z-D.

Cabernet White

(Cabernet Sauvignon Blanc)

Look for: Konocti Cellars, Montevina, Ballard Canyon, J. Carey.

CADENASSO WINERY

1955 W. Texas St., Fairfield, CA 94553

Solano County

Storage: Oak, redwood, st. steel.

President and Winemaker, Frank Cadenasso; recommended, Grignolino; vineyards, 145 acres in Suisun Valley.

CADLOLO WINERY

1124 California Street, Escalon, CA 95320

San Joaquin County

Storage: Oak, redwood and st. steel   (continued)

Owners, Ray and Ted Cadlolo. Winemaker is William Telfair. The current owners are the fourth generation at the winery.

CAKEBREAD CELLARS
8300 St. Helena Highway, Rutherford, CA 94573
Napa County
Storage: French oak barrels and st. steel
Owners, Jack and Dolores Cakebread; winemaker, Bruce Cakebread. The vineyard is located at the winery. Grapes are also purchased from select vineyards south of Yountville (Chardonay), Howell Mountain (Zinfandel) and the Stag's Leap Area (some Cabernet). 100% varietal, vintage-dated wines produced are: Sauvignon Blanc, Chardonnay, Cabernet Sauvignon (Napa Valley) and Zinfandel.

CALAVERAS CELLARS
(See Stevenot Winery)

CALAVERAS WINERY
Calaveras County
Sierra Foothills
Wines to look for: Chispa Cellars, Stevenot Vineyards.

CALERA WINE COMPANY
11300 Cienega Road, Hollister, CA 95023
San Benito County
Storage: Oak barrels
The owners are Josh and Jeanne Jensen. The winemaker is Josh Jensen. Winery is the first and only gravity-flow winery. Built on site of old limestone quarry (calera in Spanish). The vineyard is south of Hollister at 2200 feet elevation in the Gavilan Mountains. Zinfandel grapes are purchased on a select vineyard basis. Pinot Noir from their own vineyards.

Varietal, vintage-dated wines produced are "Templeton", Zinfandel, "Cienega" Zinfandel, "Doe Mill" Zinfandel, "Reed" Pinot Noir, "Selleck" Pinot Noir and "Jensen" Pinot Noir. Names indicate separate vineyard entities.

CALIFORNIA CELLAR MASTERS
212 W. Pine St., Lodi, CA 95240
San Joaquin County
President, Marcus E. Stark; Winemaker, Dennis Alexander. Grapes are purchased on a selected vineyard district basis. Varietal wines produced under the "Coloma Cellars" label are Green Hungarian, Chardonnay, Gewurztraminer, Johannisberg Riesling, Zinfandel, Gamay Beaujolais, Napa Gamay, Pinot Noir and Cabernet Sauvignon. Also produced are Blanc, Rosé, Rouge, Champagne, Sherry and Port. Under the "Gold Mine" label—burgundy and fruit wines are produced.

CALIFORNIA GROWERS WINERY
38558 Road 128, Cutler, CA 93615
Tulare County
Storage: Oak barrels and st. steel
Owner, Robert Setrakian. Family owned since 1936. Vineyard at winery and grapes are purchased from grow-

ers in selected districts. A major bulk producer and private labeler, particularly with Brandy.

Varietal wines produced are: Chenin Blanc, French Colombard, Petite Sirah, Cabernet Sauvignon and Johannisberg Riesling. Also produced are: Chablis, Burgundy, Vin Rosé, Emerald Riesling, Sherry and Cream Sherry.

California Wine
Wine produced 100% in California from grapes grown within the State.

CALIFORNIA WINE COMPANY
2211-14th St., San Francisco, CA 94103
San Francisco County
Owner, Tony Di Bono. Produced under labels: Pride of California, Champagne, Louis 5th.

California Wine Trade Beginning
Commercial wine-growing was started about 1824 by Joseph Champman, one of the first Americans to settle in California. At the Pueblo of Los Angeles, he set out about 4,000 vines. In 1831, Jean Louis Vignes, a Frenchman from the Bordeaux wine district, started a commercial vineyard approximately where the Los Angeles Union Station now stands, importing cuttings of different varieties of grapes direct from Europe. Other plantings soon followed, and within a generation winegrowing was the principal agricultural industry of the Los Angeles district. By 1840, Vignes was chartering ships which he loaded at San Pedro with wines and brandies destined for Santa Barbara, Monterey and San Francisco. As early as 1860, California wine firms had established agencies in New York and shipped wines around Cape Horn to the Eastern States. The first transcontinental railroad, in 1869, opened the remainder of the country to the wine firms. Soon California wine growers were shipping wines to Europe, Latin America and Australia. Records show that Germany, Denmark, England and Canada were buying California Port, in 1867.

CALLAWAY VINEYARD & WINERY
32720 Rancho California Road, Temecula, CA 92390
Riverside County
Storage: American, French and German oak, st. steel.
The owner is Ely Callaway.
Winemaker is Steve O'Donnell. The vineyards are located at winery. Wines are produced from grapes grown on vinifera root stock.
Wines produced are 100% varietal, estate bottled and vintage dated. They are Fume Blanc, Chenin Blanc—Dry, Sauvignon Blanc—Dry, Zinfandel, Cabernet Sauvignon, Petite Sirah, "Santana" Riesling (White Riesling), "Sweet Nancy" (Chenin Blanc). Also Callaway Port (a blend of Petite Sirah, Zinfandel and Cabernet Sauvignon).

CAMBIASO VINEYARDS
1141 Grant Avenue, Healdsburg, CA 95448
Sonoma County
Storage: Oak, redwood and st. steel   *(continued)*

The owner is the Four Seas Investment Co. The wine-maker is Robert Fredson. Old country house built in 1852 which later became residence of Cambiaso family still stands. The vineyard is located at the winery.

Varietal, vintage-dated wines produced are Chenin Blanc, Sauvignon Blanc, Cabernet Sauvignon, Petite Sirah, Zinfandel and Barbera. Under the "1852 House Wine" label, Burgundy, Chablis and Vin Rosé are produced.

J. CAREY CELLARS

1711 Alamo Pintado Road, Solvang, CA 93463
Santa Barbara County
Storage: French Limousin and Nevers oak, American oak, st. steel
Owners, Carey Family; Winemaker, Richard Longoria; Vineyards are in Santa Ynez Valley. Varietal wines produced are Cabernet Sauvignon, Merlot, Cabernet Sauvignon Blanc, Sauvignon Blanc and Chardonnay. 90% of wines are estate-bottled.

RICHARD CAREY WINERY

1695 Martinez St., San Leandro, CA 94577
Alameda County
Storage: Oak barrels, redwood and st. steel tanks
Owners, Richard and June Carey Family and friends; winemaker, Richard Carey. The grapes are purchased on a select vineyard basis—predominantly Amador and San Luis Obispo county.

Varietal, vintage-dated wines produced are: Blanc Fumé, Chardonnay, Pinot Blanc, Dry Semillion, Colombard Blanc, White Zinfandel, Red Zinfandel (Amador and San Luis Obispo Counties), Merlot, Pinot Noir, Cabernet Blanc, Cabernet Sauvignon Gewurztraminer (regular and Late Harvest) and French Colombard.

Also produced is: Burgundy Blanc and Sweet Amanda (a blend of Semillion, Gewurztraminer and Johannisberg Riesling). The winemaker's favorite wines are: Amador Zinfandel, Burgundy Blanc, Sweet Amanda and Late Harvest Gewurztraminer.

Carignane

(Red Table Wine)
A varietal grape that is predominantly used for blending. Full of tannic and heavy-bodied. Goes well with hearty meals. Originally from the Mediterranean region of Europe. Serve with hamburger, stews and Mediterranean foods. Labels to look for: Bruce, Fetzer, Oakville, Parducci, Ridge, Simi, Sycamore Creek (Vintage), Trentandue.

CARMEL BAY WINERY

P.O. Box 2496, Carmel CA 93921
Monterey County
Storage: Oak barrels
Founded 1977; Owners and winemakers are Fred Crummy and Bob Eyerman.
Varietal, vintage dated wine produced is Zinfandel.

Carnelian

A new grape variety developed by University of California at Davis. A cross between Cabernet Sauvignon, Grenache and Carignane. Yields a zesty, robust wine with complex aroma. Produced by: Giumarra Vineyards.

CARNEROS CREEK WINERY
1285 Dealy Lane, Napa, CA 94558

Napa County

Storage: American, French, German oak and st. steel

Owners are Balfour and Anita Gibson, Francis and Kathleen Mahoney. The winemaker is Frances Mahoney. The vineyard is located in Rutherford. Grapes are also purchased on a select vineyard basis from Amador and Sonoma County. 100% varietal, vintage-dated wines produced are: Cabernet Sauvignon, Pinot Noir, Zinfandel, Chardonnay, Sauvignon Blanc and Pinot Noir-Blanc. Under the "Liberty School" label a Cabernet Sauvignon is produced. The Winemaker's favorite wines are Cabernet Sauvignon and Pinot Noir.

CASSAYRE-FORNI CELLARS
1271 Manley Lane, Rutherford, CA 94573

Napa County

Storage: Oak and st. steel

Owners are Jim and Paul Cassayre, Mike Forni and Frank Mahoney. The winemaker is Mike Forni.

Grapes are purchased on a selected grower and district basis. Varietal wines produced are Napa Valley Chenin Blanc, Napa Valley Cabernet Sauvignon and Sonoma County (Dry Creek Valley) Zinfandel. Winemakers favorite wine is Sonoma County Zinfandel.

CAVALCADE
(See Emilio Gugliemo Winery)

C. C. VINEYARD
(See J. F. J. Bronco Winery)

Chablis
A dry, white dinner or table wine, Chablis has a fruity flavor, but less tart than Rhine. It is delicate, light to medium straw in color and light to medium-bodied. Good with white meats and seafood.

CHALONE VINEYARD
P.O. Box 855, Soledad, CA 93960

Monterey County

Owner, Gavilon Vineyards; president, W. Philip Woodward; Winemaker, Peter Watson-Graff. The vineyard was founded in 1919. The winery was established in 1960. The vineyard is near the Pinnacles National Monument at 2,000 feet elevation. Varietal, vintage-dated, Estate-bottled wines produced are: Pinot Noir, Chardonnay, Pinot Blanc, and Chenin Blanc, French Colombard is also produced in the style of the Estate-bottled wines.

Champagne Bottle Sizes
"Split": 187 ml or 6.4 oz, single serving, convenient for Champagne Cocktails.

"Tenth": 375 ml or 12.8 oz, serves two.

"Fifth": 750 ml or 25.4 oz, four to five servings.

"Magnum": 1.5 liters or 51 oz.

"Double Magnum": 3 liters for celebrations.

Champagne, "Bulk Process" Method

"Bulk Process" involves fermenting wine in large tanks and filtering and bottling in the same manner as the transfer process. This product *must* carry the designation "Charmat" or "Bulk Process" on the label. Less expensive California sparkling wines are produced by this method.

Champagne Production "Naturally Fermented in *This* Bottle" French: Methode Champenoise

The individual bottle-fermented method in which every stage of production takes place in the individual bottle, and the resulting product reaches the consumer in its original container. This process is referred to as the "Traditional Method." By law, only Champagne produced by this method may bear the inscription "NATURALLY FERMENTED IN *THIS* BOTTLE."

The first fermentation in the bottle is the art of the Champagne Cellarmaster or Winemaker. Before bottling the blended wines that are destined for Champagne, it is necessary to add the exact amount of sugar in order to produce-supported by addition of a very active, pure cultured yeast—6 atmospheres of carbon dioxide at a temperature of 50°. The carbon dioxide makes the wine sparkling as soon as the fermentation in the bottle has finished.

The bottles are stacked in cool cellars of equitable temperature, where they await ripening and bottle-aging. At regular intervals the bottles are removed and shaken in order to avoid having the sediment— produced by the fermentation—stick to the sides of the bottles.

After storage and aging of several years, the Champagne is placed on racks with holes for the necks of the bottles, which are always directed downward. Each bottle is shaken and turned, alternately, in the right and left direction, at regular intervals during a period of 8 – 10 weeks, until the sediment has settled on the cork of the downwardly-directed bottle, and the wine is absolutely transparent.

Only 3 – 6 months before shipment takes place, the Champagne is freed from the sediment. For this purpose, the bottles with their heads placed downwards, are brought into a freezing solution and cooled below 12° F. A few minutes of this immersion are sufficient to freeze the sediment and a small amount of the wine onto the cork. It is now possible to turn the bottle upright, and to get the cork out of the bottle, which is blown out of the neck, together with the sediment, with force. The pressure forces the cork out carrying the frozen sediment with it.

Before the second finishing cork is put into the bottle, a small additional dosage is added. The finest cane sugar is dissolved in an excellent old, well-balanced wine, and the best quality of aged grape brandy makes this dosage perfect. This creation of the dosage and the amount is the art of the Winemaker. The "style" reflects the individual Winemaker. The quantity of the dosage depends on the taste to suit the consumer. For Brut there is no addition of dosage.   *(continued)*

Special heavy bottles made to withstand pressure of 6 –8 atmospheres and only finest corks available are used. After being disgorged, the Champagne is stored for several months before being made available for shipment.

Look for these Champagnes: Alamaden Blanc de Blanc, Beaulieu Blanc de Chardonnay, Domaine Chandon Pinot Noir Brut, Domaine Chandon Brut, Schramsberg Blanc De Noir Brut, Schramsberg Blanc de Blanc, Schramsberg Cureé de Gamay, Korbel "Natural", Paul Masson Johannisberg Riesling, Beaulieu, Hans Kornell Sehr Trocken, Hans Kornell Brut, Sonoma Blanc de Blanc, Korbel Blanc de Noirs, Chateau St. Jean Blanc de Noir, Mirrassou, Weibel.

Champagne, "Transfer Method"

The "Transfer Method" is a variation on the traditional method, which involves fermenting the Champagne in the bottle, thus qualifying for a "FERMENTED IN *THE* BOTTLE" label designation. After fermenting in the bottle, however, the contents are removed under counterpressure and placed in large pressurized tanks, mechanically filtered into another tank, and then refilled into empty bottles. Method used for medium priced Champagnes. Look for: Le Domain, Weibel, Cristian Brothers, Paul Masson.

Charbono

(Red Table Wine)

A varietal grape that means a full-bodied, distinct tannic, robust, earthy wine. Very few acres planted in California. Originally from Italy. Fuller bodied than Barbera. Serve with stews and robust Italian foods. Ages very well. (Best at 4 to 6 years.) Look for these Charbonos: Inglenook, Davis Bynum, Papagni, Fortino, Souverain.

CHAPPELLET VINEYARD

1581 Sage Canyon Road, St. Helena, CA 94574

Napa County

Storage: Oak and st. steel

Founded 1969; Owner, Donn Chappellet, winemaker is Tony Soter.

Vineyard, 100 acres. Varietal vintage dated wines produced are Cabernet Sauvignon, Gamay, Chenin Blanc, Johannisberg Riesling and Chardonnay. Known for superb cabernet sold to mailing list only.

Character

The wine's "personality" as revealed by the senses of taste and smell. The combination of vinosity, balance and style.

Chardonnay

(White Table Wine)

A varietal grape that produces a prestigious wine, whether it be in California, or in one of the great white Burgundy wine-producing districts of France.

Full-bodied with medium acidity. A dry austere wine with a slight or faint flavor reminiscent of applies, melons or figs. Bright, crisp and complex.

Magnificent with a wide range of "white" foods, including rich cream sauces, or enjoyed simply with fruit, crackers and cheese—Brie or Camenbert. Currently California's most expensive wine grape. Look for these Chardonnays: David Bruce, Burgess, Beaulieu, Chalone, Chappellett, Conn Creek, Cuvaison, Chateau St. Jean, Chateau Montelena, Clos De Bois, Chateau Chevalier, Christian Bros., Chateau Montelena, Dry Creek, Dehlinger, Firestone, Freemark Abbey, Fetzer, Husch, Hacienda "Claire de Lune", Hoffman Mountain Ranch (HMR), Heitz), Hanzell, Iron Horse, Jekel, Kenwood, Keenan, LaCrema (Winery Lake), J. Lohr, Long, Robert Mondavi, Mayacamas, Mark West, Mill Creek, Monterey Vineyard, Mount Eden, Mount Veeder, Martin Ray, Paul Masson Pinnacles, Mirassou, Matanzas, Pope Valley, Ridge, Raymond, Rutherford Hill, Simi, Stag's Leap Wine Cellars, Santa Ynez Valley, Stonegate, Sterling, Smith Madrone, Spring Mountain, Sonoma, San Martin, St. Clement, Stony Hill, Villa Mt. Eden, Wente Bros, Z-D.

CHATEAU CHEVALIER WINERY

3101 Spring Mountain Road, St. Helena, CA 94574
Napa County
Storage: French oak and st. steel

Owners, Greg and Kathy Bissonette; Winemaker, Greg Bissonette. The vineyard was originally planted in the late 1870s. The vineyard is located at the winery on Spring Mountain Road. Varietal, Estate-bottled wines produced under Chateau Chevalier label are: Cabernet Sauvignon, Chardonnay, Merlot, Pinot Noir and White Riesling.

Varietal wines produced under the Mountainside Vineyards label, from purchased graps are: Cabernet Sauvignon, Chardonnay, Merlot and Zinfandel. Favorite wine of the Winemaker is the Private Reserve Cabernet Sauvignon, vintage dated.

CHATEAU MOREAU

(See Gibson Wine Co.)

CHATEAU MONTELENA

1429 Tubbs Lane, Calistoga, CA 94515
Napa County
Storage: French oak

Owners, James L. Barrett, Lee J. Paschich and Ernest W. Hahn; Winemaker, Jerry Luper. The vineyards are located at the winery in the Napa Valley.

Founded in 1882 by Alfred L. Tubbs, who was a State Senator, Builder and Owner of a whaling fleet, the Chateau was designed by a French architect and built of local and imported stone. The current Owners took over in 1972. The most significant award that set the wine world on its ear took place at the "Paris Tasting," in 1976. Chateau Montelena's 1973 Chardonnay was awarded first place over nine other top French White Burgundies, and California Chardonnays in a blind tasting. The tasting panel was comprised of nine of France's "Who's Who" of the wine world.

The varietal, vintage-dated wines produced are: Johannisberg Riesling, Chardonnay, Zinfandel and Cabernet Sauvignon. The Winemaker's favorite wine is Cabernet Sauvignon.

CHATEAU NAPOLEON
(See Weibel Champagne Vineyards)

CHATEAU ST. JEAN
8555 Sonoma Highway, Kenwood, CA 95452
Sonoma County
Storage: American and French oak, st. steel
Owners, Robert and Edward Merzonian and W. Kenneth Sheffield. The President is Allan J. Hemphill. The Winemaker is Richard L. Arrowood. The vineyards are located at the winery. The grapes are also purchased from select vineyards in Napa, Sonoma, and Mendocino Counties.

Varietal, vintage-dated wines produced are: Alexander Valley Johannisberg Riesling, Sonoma County Johannisberg Riesling (Selected Late Harvest), Alexander Valley Johhanisberg Riesling (Late Harvest), Northern Coast Johannisberg Riesling, Alexander Valley Gewurztraminer (Individual Bunch-Selected Late Harvest), Sonoma County Gewurztraminer.

Chenin Blanc
A widely planted white grape essential to the popular jug, white wines now consumed as cocktails. It yeilds a variety of different types and quality of wine subject to where it is grown and the intention of the winemaker. Usually associated with a lovely, fruity, aromatic "feminine" wine with slight residual sweetness. Usually drank as a social wine rather than a dinner wine but it is quite appropriate with Chinese or Polynesian food. There are some dry versions that are more suitable table wines. Look for these Chenin Blanc's: Bargetto, Burgess, Casseyri-Forni, Chappellet, Callaway-Dry, Chalone, Cuvaison, Dry Creek, Durney, Charles Krug, Kenwood-Dry, Franciscan, Hoffman Mt. Ranch, J. Lohr, Mirrasou, Mt. Veeder, Robert Mondavi, Parducci, Papagni "Sparkling Chenin", Raymond, San Pasqual, San Martin, Sonoma, Sterling, Stag's Leap Vineyard, Simi, Souverain, Wente 'Blanc de Blanc'.

CHISPA CELLARS
P.O. Box 255, Murphys, CA 95247
Calaveras County
Owners and winemakers are Robert Bliss and Riggs. Grapes are purchased on a select vineyard basis. Wines produced are Ruby Cabernet and Zinfandel.

CHRISTIAN BROTHERS
4411 Redwood Road, Napa CA 94558
Napa County
Storage: Oak, redwood and st. steel
The Owner is The Christian Brothers, a Catholic order of men devoted to teaching. Over 15,000 Christian Brothers teach in over 1,600 schools in 80 countries. Profits from the wines are used to support these schools. The winemaker is David Cofran. Brother Timothy is

Cellarmaster. The Christian Brothers own vast vineyards in the Napa Valley and the San Joaquin Valley.

The wines produced are: Brother Timothy Special Selection, varietal Zinfandel, Pinot Noir, Gamay Noir and Cabernet Sauvignon. Napa Valley varietals: Cabernet Sauvignon, Zinfandel, Gamay Noir, Pinot Noir, Estate-bottled. Pinot St. George, Johannisberg Riesling, Grey Riesling, Chenin Blanc, Napa Fumé (Sauvignon Blanc), Pineau de la Loire, Pinot, Chardonnay and Riesling. Mont La Salle is a label devoted to limited release Estate-bottled vintage-dated varietal wines. They are: Pinot St. George, Cabernet Sauvignon and Chardonnay.

Generic wines are: Chablis, Rhine, Sauterne, Burgundy and Claret. Also, Napa Rosé, Vin Rosé, La Salle Rosé and Chateau La Salle, Sherries are: Meloso Cream, Cocktail, Dry, Golden and Cream. Ports are: Tinta Cream, Treasure, Tawny and Ruby. Amber Tokay and Golden Muscatel are produced in addition to Brut and Extra Dry Champagne, Champagne Rosé, Extra Cold Duck and Sparkling Burgundy.

CILURZON AND PICONI

41220 Calle Contento, Temecula, CA 92390
Riverside County
Storage: Oak barrels and st. steel
Owners and Winemakers, Vincenzo Cilurzo and Dr. John Piconi. The vineyard is located in Temecula. The varietal, Estate-bottled wines produced are: Cabernet Sauvignon and Petite Sirah. The Winemaker's favorite wine is Petite Sirah.

Claret

Claret applies to any dry pleasantly-tart, light and medium-bodied dinner wine of ruby-red color. Originated by the British to describe acceptable Bordeaux wines. This is the most widely-used mealtime wine in the world. In California, Clarets are made from one, or more, of a number of grape varieties, such as Cabernet Sauvignon, Zinfandel and Merlot.

CLOS DU BOIS

764 West Dry Creek Road, Healdsburg, CA 95448
Sonoma County
Storage: American and French oak, st. steel
Owner, Frank Montgomery Woods; Winemaker, Tom Hobart. The vineyards are located in Dry Creek Valley and Alexander Valley. The first vintage wines were released in 1976, and a medal winner at National and International tasting competitions.

Varietal, Estate-bottled, vintage-dated wines produced are: Chardonnay, Gewurztraminer, Johannisberg Riesling, Pinot Noir and Cabernet Sauvignon. Recommended: Cabernet Sauvignon, Proprieter's Reserve.

CLOS DU VAL

5330 Silverado Trail, Napa, CA 94558
Napa County
Storage: Oak tanks and barrels
Founded 1973; Owner and Winemaker, Bernard M. Portet. *(continued)*

The vineyard is located near the winery. Bernard Portet was raised in Pauillac, France, and is the son of the Regisseur of Chateau Lafite Rothschild.

The vintage-dated varietal wines produced under the Clos Du Val and Grandval labels are: Cabernet Sauvignon, Zinfandel and Chardonnay.

COARSEGOLD WINE CELLAR
Highway #41, Coarsegold, CA 93614
Madera County
Owner, H. A. Button

COAST RANGE NEGOCIANTS
32 Woodland Avenue, San Rafael, CA 94901
Coast Range offers two releases: 100% varietal, vintage dated San Luis Obispo Chardonnay and Alexander Valley Cabernet Sauvignon.

Cold Duck
A blend of White Champagne and Sparkling Burgundy and a little Concord grape wine. Cold Duck is semi-sweet to sweet and is ruby-red in color. It is a light and festive wine, traditional in Germany and enjoying success recently during the "Pop Wine" trend in the U.S.

COLOMA CELLARS
McHenery Aven., Escalon, CA
San Joaquin County
(See California Cellar Masters) Branch tasting room of original winery in Coloma California. Site of Gold discovery.

COLONY
(Italian Swiss)
P.O. Box One, Asti, California 95413
Sonoma County
(see United Vintners)
Owner, United Vintners; Winemaker, Ed Rossi, Jr. Formerly known as Italian Swiss Colony which was formed as a mutual Association, in 1881. United Vintners purchased the property in the late 1960s. Varietal wines produced are: French Comombard, Chenin Blanc, Rhine, Riesling, Cabernet Sauvignon, Pinot Noir, Zinfandel, Barbera and Ruby Cabernet. Also produced are: Chablis, Rhine, Sauterne Blanc, Rhineskeller, Moselle, Grenache Vin Rosé, Burgundy, Chianti, Sherry and Port.

COLUMBIA CELLARS
(See Yankee Hill Winery)

CONCANNON VINEYARD
4590 Tesla Road, Livermore, CA 94550
Alameda County
Storage: Oak and st. steel
The Owner is Augustin Huneeus. The Winemaker is Robert Broman. Founded in 1883 by James Concannon, the vineyard is located in the Livermore Valley. The first winery in America to produce Petite Sirah. Varietal, vintage-dated wines produced are: Chenin Blanc, Sauvignon Blanc, Johannisberg Riesling, Muscat Blanc, Chateau Concannon (Semillon), Petite Sirah, Amador

County Zinfandel (100%), Cabernet Sauvignon and vintage-dated Zinfandel Rosé.

Also produced are: Rkatsiteli (the only winery in America to produce this), Burgundy, Chablis and Moselle.

The Winemaker's favorite wines are: Petite Sirah, Sauvignon Blanc and Rkatsiteli.

CONN CREEK WINERY
8711 Silverado Trail, St. Helena, CA 94574
Napa County
Storage: French oak and st. steel
The Owners are Bill and Kathy Collins and Bill and May Beaver. The Winemaker is John Henderson. There are two vineyards in the Napa Valley.

Estate-bottled, varietal wines produced are: Napa Valley Cabernet Sauvignon, Napa Valley Zinfandel, Napa Valley Chardonnay, Napa Valley Johannisberg Riesling and Chateau Maja (2/3) Chardonnay, 1/3 Johannisberg Riesling). Favorite wines of the Winemaker are: Cabernet Sauvignon and Zinfandel.

CONGRESS SPRINGS VINEYARDS
23600 Congress Springs Road, Saratoga, CA 95070
Santa Clara County
Storage: Oak and st. steel
The Owners are Vic Erickson and Dan Gehrs. The Winemaker is Dan Gehrs. The winery was founded in the 1890s by a French immigrant Pierre C. Pourroy. The current owners first crush was in 1976. Vineyard is in Santa Cruz Mountains of Santa Clara County.

Varietal, vintage-dated wines produced are Pinot Blanc, Fumé Blanc, Semillon, Chenin Blanc, Chardonnay, Gewurztraminer, Cabernet Sauvignon, Cabernet Franc, Zinfandel and Pinot Noir. The Winemaker's favorite wines are Pinot Noir.

CONROTTO WINERY ANSELMO
1690 Hecker Pass Highway, Gilroy, CA 95020
Santa Clara County
Owner, Anselmo Concotto

CONTI ROYALE
(See East-Side Winery)

CONTRA COSTA COUNTY
(Inland North Central Coast)
CONRAD VIANO WINERY
J.J. Digardi Winery

Controlled Fermentation
The most common method is refrigeration. The aim is to speed up or slow down the process, as needed and prevent excessive heat which might cause oxidation or damage to the delicate flavors of the wine.

R. & J. COOK
Netherlands Road, Clarksburg, CA 95612
Yolo County
Storage: American and French oak, st. steel
Owners, Roger and Joanne Cook; Winemaker, Bruce McGuire. The vineyards are in regions unknown to most

people and is another unique microclimate region. The vineyards are in Clarksburg and Solano. Varietal, Estate-bottled, vintage-dated wines produced are: Chenin Blanc, Rosé of Petite Sirah, Cavernet Sauvignon, Blanc de Noir of Cabernet, Merlot and Napa Gamay.

Cooperage
The general term used to designate containers in which wines are stored and aged. It includes casks and wooden or stainless steel aging tanks. The term derives from the occupation of cooper—one who makes or repairs wooden containers. The cooper's art has recently been revived in Northern California where several small shops assemble, repair and shave fine oak barrels from Europe. The actual manufacture of small American Oak barrels is still limited to Missouri and Arkansas.

COPENHAGEN CELLARS—VIKINGS FOUR
448 Alisal Road, Solvang, CA 93463
Santa Barbara County
Owner, Donovan Gauthier

CORTI BROTHERS
5760 Freeport Blvd, Sacramento, CA 95822
Highly regarded retailers who select and have wines finished to their specifications. Stony Hill Semillon de Soleil is produced exclusively for Corti Bros. The strip label indicates this.

CONSUMNES RIVER VINEYARD
(See Story Vineyards)

H. COTURRI & SON, LTD.
P.O. Box 396, Glen Ellen, CA 95442
Sonoma County
Founded 1979, Owned by Harry, Tony and Phillip Cotturi. Tony is the winemaker and Phillip the vineyard manager. Phillip is also a vineyard developer by profession. First releases Dec. 1980, Semillion and Riesling. In 1981 they will release Chardonnay, Zinfandel and Cabernet Sauvignon from select vineyards.

Cremant
Champagne that is about one-half the standard effervescene.

CRESTA BELLA
(See Gibson Wine Co.)

CRESTA BLANCA
(See Guild Wineries)

CRIBARI
(See Guild Wineries)

Cru
A vineyard or growth

Crush
The process of stemming and crushing grapes for wine at harvest time. The purpose is to break the skins and release the juice. Not to be confused with pressing which comes later.

Crust
Deposit of sediment by wine while aging in the bottle;

the deposit adheres to the inside of the bottle as a crust. Crusted wines are old, bottle-aged.

CRYSTAL SPRINGS
(See Pedrizzetti Winery)

CUCAMONGA VINEYARDS
10013-8th Street, Rancho Cucamonga, CA 91730
San Bernardino County
Storage: Oak, redwood and st. steel
Owner, Philo Pierre Biane; Winemaker, Primo F. Scorsatto. The Biane Family is a sixth-generation California wine-making family.

Wines produced are: Limited Edition Brut and Extra Dry Champagnes, Moscato Spumante, Cuvee d'Or Extra Dry Champagne, Pink Champagne, Sparkling Burgundy, Cold Duck, Chablis, Rosé, Burgundy, Cabernet, Sauvignon, Chenin Blanc, Petite Sirah, Johannisberg Riesling and Moscato De Primo.

The Winemaker's favorite wines are: the Limited Edition Champagnes and Moscato Spumante.

CUCAMONGA VINTNERS
10277 Foothill Blvd., Cucamonga, CA 91730
President, Arthur Accomazzo

Cutting
In vitaculture, a segment of the cane or branch of a grapevine cut during the dormant season and used for propogation of new vines. Most new grapevines are planted as cuttings—rarely as seeds.

CUVAISON
4560 Silverado Trail, Calistoga, CA 94515
Napa County
Storage: French oak and st. steel
The Owner is Stefan Schmideiny. The Winemaker is Philip Togni. The vineyard is at Carneros on a hillside in the Napa Valley.

Varietal, vintage-dated, Estate-bottled wines produced are: Chardonnay, Cabernet Sauvignon and Zinfandel.

The Winemaker's favorite wine is Cabernet Sauvignon.

Cuveé
Literally, the contents of a cask of wind—usually refers to an especially-prepared blend of wines such as a blend of still wines before secondary fermentation, to produce Champagne.

CUVEÉ d'OR
(See Cucamoga Vineyard Co.)

CYGNET CELLARS
11736 Cienega Road, Hollister, CA 95023
San Benito County
Storage: Oak barrels
The Owner is Jim Johnson. The Winemaker is Cliff Hight. The grapes are purchased from a vineyard in San Luis Obispo County. Varietal, vintage-dated wines produced are: Zinfandel, petite Sirah and Chardonnay (Late Harvest), Carignane Natural Port (unfortified 19.6% Alcohol), Palomino Dry Sherry and Cabernet Sauvignon.

The Winemaker's favorite wines are: Zinfandel and Carignane Port.

D

DACH VINEYARDS
9200 Highway 128, Philo, CA 95466
Mendocino County
The Owners are John and Sandi Dach. The Winemaker is John Dach, the vineyard is located at the winery.

The wines, as they become available, will be sold at the Dach fruit stand.

Wines to be produced are: Pinot Chardonnay, Gewurztraminer, Pinot Noir and Apple.

D'AGOSTINI WINERY
Shenandoah Road, Plymouth, CA
Amador County
Founded 1856; Winemaker, Tulio D'Agostini. Recommended: Estate-bottled Zinfandel and Dry Museat.

Decant
To pour wine gently from the bottle in which crust or sediment has been deposited, for the purpose of obtaining clear wine for serving. The container into which the wine is poured is called a decanter. Decant also means to pour wine from a large container into a small container for more convenient handling.

DEER PARK WINERY
1000 Deer Park Road, Deer Park, CA 94576
Napa County
Storage: French oak and st. steel.
Owners, David and Kinta Clark, Lila and Robert Knapp; Winemaker, David Clark; Vineyard, 7 acres.

Varietal wines produced are Zinfandel and Chardonnay.

DEHLINGER WINERY
6300 Guerneville Road, Sebastopol, CA 95472
Sonoma County
Founded 1976; Owners, Tom and Klaus Dehlinger; Winemaker, Tom Dehlinger; Vineyard, 14 acres.

DELICATO VINEYARDS
12001 So. Highway 99, Manteca, CA 95336
San Joaquin County
Storage: Oak, redwood and st. steel.
The Owners are Anthony, Frank and Vincent Indelicato. The Winemaker is Hector Castro. The vineyards were planted in 1924 by two brothers-in-law, Gaspare Indelicato and Sebastiano Luppino. The winery was started in 1935. The vineyards are located at the winery and in the Clements area.

Varietal wines produced are: Johannisberg Riesling, Pinot Chardonnay, Green Hungarian, Chenin Blanc, French Colombard, Grenache Rosé, Zinfandel, Cabernet Sauvignon, Gamay Beaujolais, Pinot Noir, Barbera and Petite Sirah.

Also produced are: Chablis, Chablis Blanc, Rhine, Vin

Rosé, Burgundy, Chianti, Champagne, Pink Champagne, Cold Duck, Sherry and Port. The Winemaker's favorites are: Green Hungarian, French Colombard, Petite Sirah, Cabernet Sauvignon and Grenache Rosé.

CECIL DE LOACH VINEYARDS

1791 Olivet Road, Santa Rosa, CA 95401
Sonoma County
Storage: Oak and st. steel
Owners, Cecil and Christine De Loach; Winemaker, Larry Wara and Cecil De Loach; Vineyards, 53 acres. The vineyard is located at the winery in the Russian River Valley, 100% varietal, vintage-dated, Estate-bottled wines produced are: White Zinfandel, Zinfandel and Pinot Noir-Blanc.

Also produced are: vintage-dated, varietal Sonoma County, Gewurztraminer, Lytton Springs Zinfandel and Pinot Noir.

Demi-Sec

Fairly sweet.

Dessert Wines

Sweet, full-bodied wines served with desserts or as refreshments, are called dessert wines. Their alcohol content is 18% – 21%. They range from medium-sweet to sweet and from pale gold to red. The three distinct popular types, in addition to Sherry, are: Port, Muscatel and Tokay. Dessert Wines: Angelica, Madeira, Marsala, Muscatel, Port, Sherry and Tokay.

DEVLIN WINE CELLARS

P.O. Box 723, Soquel, CA 95073
Santa Cruz County
Storage: American and French oak, st. steel.
The Owner and Winemaker is Charles Devlin. The grapes are purchased on a selected region basis.

Varietal, vintage-dated wines produced are: Livermore Valley Zinfandel, Sonoma County Chardonnay and Monterey County Chardonnay.

DIABLO VISTA WINERY

674 E. "H" St., Benicia, CA 94510
The Owners are L.K. Borowski and K. I. Blodgett. Varietal wines produced are: Cabernet Sauvignon, Zinfandel, Pinot Noir and Pinot Chardonnay.

DIAMOND CREEK VINEYARDS

1500 Diamond Mountain Road, Calistoga, CA 94515
Napa County
Storage: Nevers oak barrels
Founded 1972. The Owner and Winemaker is Al Brounstein. The vineyard is located at the winery. 90% is planted in Cabernet Sauvignon and 10% in Merlot. Diamond Creek produces only Cabernet Sauvignon. The vineyard is divided into 3 areas and the label indicates either Red Rock Terrace, Volanic Hill or Gravelly Meadow, each with its own personality.

J. E. DIGARDI WINERY

3785 Pacheco Blvd., Martinez, CA 94553
Contra Costa County
Owner, Francis J. Digardi; Vineyard, 1 acre.

Dinner Wine

(See Table Wine)

DOMAINE CHANDON

California Drive, Yountville, CA 94599

Napa County

Storage: St. steel.

Domaine Chandon is a wholly-owned subsidiary of Moet-Hennessy, a French Company that owns Champagne Moet and Chandon, Hennessy Cognac and Dior Perfumes—the first French-owned vineyards in America. The President is John Wright. The winemaker is Edmond Maudiere (Moet and Chandon, France). The vineyards are located on Mt. Veeder, Carneros district and at the winery. They specialize in sparkling wines.

Two sparkling wines are produced—Chandon Napa Valley Brut (Pinot Noir, Chardonnay and Pinot Blanc) and Chandon Blanc de Noirs (Pinot Noir).

The Winemaker's favorite wines are: Napa Valley, Brut and Blanc de Noirs. They also produce an interesting aperitif made of Pinot Noir called "Panache."

Dosage

The addition of sugared wine and brandy to another wine in order to make it conform to established standards of dryness. Only used for Champagne and sparkling wines.

Dry

The opposite of sweet; free of sugar. Fermentation converts the natural sugar of the grape into wine alcohol and carbon dioxide gas. A wine becomes dry when all the sugar has been consumed by fermentation. Dryness should not be confused with astringency, acidity, tartness or sourness; it simply means lacking in sweetness. The wines which uninformed individuals are apt to call "sour" are dry or tart, made with these flavor characteristics especially to blend with the flavors of main course foods. (A Champagne or Sherry labeled "dry" is actually semi-dry, and even an "extra-dry" Champagne may be slightly sweet). Really dry Champagne is labeled "Brut" or "Nature"; the driest sherries are labeled "Extra Dry."

DRY CREEK VINEYARD

3770 Lambert Bridge Road, Healdsburg, CA 95448

Sonoma County

Storage: Oak and st. steel.

The Owner and Winemaker is David S. Stare. The vineyard is located at the winery in the Dry Creek Valley. Grapes are also purchased on a select vineyard basis, from local growers.

100% varietal, vintage-dated wines produced are: Zinfandel and Cabernet Sauvignon.

Occasionally, Merlot, Petite Sirah and Gewurztraminer are produced.

DUCK HORN VINEYARDS

3027 Silverado Trail, St. Helena, CA 94574

Napa County

Winemaker, Thomas Renaldi recommends their Napa Valley Merlot.

DUDENHOEFER
(See Barengo Vineyards)

DURNEY VINEYARD
P.O. Box 1146, Carmel Valley, CA 93924
Monterey County
Storage: Oak barrels and st. steel.
The Owners are W. W. and D. K. Durney. The Wine-maker is John Estell. The vineyard is located at the winery and the only one in the Carmel Valley, at the end of the Santa Lucia range.

Varietal, vintage-dated wines produced are: Cabernet Sauvignon, Johannisberg Riesling, Chenin Blanc and Gamay Beaujolais.

DUTCHER CREEK
(See Rege Wine Co.)

E

EAST-SIDE WINERY
6100 E. Highway 12, Lodi, CA 95240
San Joaquin County
Owner is a Corporate Cooperative. The Winemaker is Lee Eichele. Varietal wines produced under the Conti-Royale label are: Chenin Blanc and Petite Sirah.

Also produced are: Tinta Madeira, Port and Cocktail Sherry.

Edelzwicker
A white wine from a blend of Gewurztraminer and White Riesling Grapes. ("Edel"—Noble, "Zwicker"—mixture or blend.)

EDMEADES VINEYARDS
5500 California State Highway #128, Philo, CA 95466
Mendocino County
Storage: American and French oak, st. steel.
The Owners are Deron Edmeades, Cecilia Schreiner and Bradford Wiley, II. The winemaker is Jedidiah T. Steele. The vineyard is located at the winery in the Anderson Valley.

Varietal wines produced are: Cabernet Sauvignon, Zinfandel, Chardonnay, Gewurztraminer and Pinot Noir.

Also produced are: Rain Wine (Generic White), Queen Anne's Lace (Generic Red), Whale Wine (Generic White), and Opal (White Pinot Noir).

The Winemamer's favorite wines are: Rain Wine, Zinfandel, Pinot Noir and Gewurztraminer.

EL DORADO COUNTY
(Sierra Foothills). Wines to look for: Boerger, Coloma Cellars, El Dorado, Sierra Vista.

EL DORADO VINEYARDS
3551 Carson Road, Camino, CA 95709
Eldorado County
The Owners are Earl and Jo Anne McGuire. The wine-maker is Earl McGuire. Varietal wines produced are: Zinfandel, Chenin Blanc, White Reisling, Pinot Noir, Chardonnay, Merlot, Sauvignon Blanc and Gamay.

Emerald Riesling (White Table Wine)

A varietal grape developed at the University of California, Davis. It is the child of Johannisberg Riesling and Muscadelle—one of the Muscat family. A light, fresh, fruity, slightly sweet wine. Excellent with poultry and shell fish. Look for: Paul Masson, Angelo Papagni (Late Harvest)

EMILE'S

(See Emilio Guglielmo Winery)

ENDGATE VINEYARDS

310 Capetown Court, Novato, CA 94947

Enology

The science of the study of winemaking; related to viticulture, which is the science of grape culture. The University of California, Davis, is the leading center in the United States.

ENZ VINEYARDS

Lime Kiln Valley, Hollister, CA 95023
San Benito County
Storage: Oak and st. steel
The Owners are Robert and Susan Enz. The Winemaker is Robert Enz. The vineyards were planted in 1895 and are still producing. They are located at the winery.

Varietal, vintage-dated wines produced are: Pinot St. George, Zinfandel, White Zinfandel, Golden Chasselas and Fumé Blanc.

ESHCOL

(See Treffethen Vineyards)

ESPIRIT

(See United Vintners)

ESTANCIA

(See Hacienda Wine Cellars)

Esters

Aromatic substances brought about by the reactions of alcohols and acids in wine, which contribute to bouquet.

ESTRELLA RIVER WINERY

Shandon Star Route, Paso Robles, CA 95446
San Luis Obispo County
Storage: American and French oak.
The Owners are Clifford R. Giacobine, Sally Giacobine, and Clifford James Giacobine.

The Winemaker, W. Gary Eberle, is also a family member. The vineyard is located at the winery. A new, but already medal-winning, winery at competitive tastings. Estate-bottled, varietal, vintage-dated wines produced are: Chenin Blanc, Sauvignon Blanc, Chardonnay, Johannisberg Riesling, Muscat Canelli, Cabernet Sauvignon, Zinfandel, Barbera and French Sirah.

EVENSEN VINEYARDS

8254 St. Helena Highway, Napa, CA 94558
Napa County
Owners, Richard and Sharen Evensen; Vineyard is located at winery in Napa Valley.
Varietal, vintage dated, Estate-Bottled wine produced is Gewurztraminer.

Extra Dry

In Champagne, slightly less dry than Brut. In Sherry, the driest.

F

FAMILY VINEYARD

(See Bella Napoli Winery)

FAR NIENTE WINERY

Oakville Grade, Oakville, CA

Napa County

Storage: Limousin oak

The Owners are Gil Nickel, Douglas Stebbing and Robert Lieff. The Winemaker is Gil Nickel. Vineyard, 20 acres. Founded in 1885 by Capt. John Benson, the winery located in Napa Valley near Oakville was renovated in recent years. Vineyards are in Napa Valley. Its first crush was in 1979. The varietal vintage dated wines produced are Chardonnay and Cabernet Sauvignon.

FARNESI WINERY

2426 Almond Ave., Sanger, CA 93657

Fresno County

Founded 1936. Owner, Danny C. Farnesi

FELTA SPRINGS

(See Mill Creek Vineyards)

FENESTRA WINERY

83 E. Vallecitos Road, Livermore, CA 94550

Alameda County

FELTON-EMPIRE VINEYARDS

379 Felton Empire Road, Felton, CA 95018

Santa Cruz County

Storage: American and French oak, st. steel

The Owners are Leo P. McCloskey, John Pollard, James Beauregard and Bill Gibbs. The Winemaker is Leo P. McCloskey. Vineyards are in three parts of Santa Cruz County, at the winery and two in the Bonny Doon District. Vineyards along the coast are also used under the copyright names, MARITIME VINEYARD SERIES and MARITIME Series.

Varietal, vintage-dated wines produced are Cabernet Sauvignon, Riesling, Gewurztraminer, Chenin Blanc and Chardonnay.

FENTON ACRES WINERY

6152 Westside Road, Healdsburg, CA 95448

Sonoma County

Storage: Oak barrels

The owners are Joe Rochioli, Jr., Gerry O'Conner and John Broschofsky. Varietal wines produced are Chardonnay and Pinot Noir.

Fermentation

The chemical process whereby sugars are broken down into alcohol carbonic acid gas, and other by-products.

FERRARA WINERY

1120 West 15th Avenue, Escondido, CA 92025

Founded 1932. The Owner is Casper D. Ferrara. The

Winemaker is George Ferrara. The family is a third-generation winemaking family.

FERREIRA WINES
5990 Wing Road, Newcastle, CA 9595
Sacramento County
Founded 1977. President, Alex Ferreira

FETZER VINEYARDS
1150 Bel Arbes Road, Redwood Valley, CA 95470
Mendocino County
The Owner is Bernard A. Fetzer. The Winemaker is Paul Dolan. Eight members of the Fetzer family work at the vineyards. Parts of the original vineyard were planted in the late 1880s. The vineyard is located near the headwaters of the Russian River. The varietal, vintage dated wines produced are: Cabernet Sauvignon, Petite Sirah, Zinfandel (Mendocino County), Zinfandel (Lake County), Gamay Beaujolais, Johannisberg Riesling, Sauvignon Blanc, Gewurztraminer, Chenin Blanc, Pinot Blanc and Chardonnay. Winemakers favorites are: 1978 Chardonnay and 1977 estate-bottled Cabernet Sauvignon.

FICKLIN VINEYARDS
30246 Avenue 7-12, Madera, CA 93637
Madera County
Owners are the Ficklin Family. David B. Ficklin and Walter C. Ficklin, Jr. First Winemaker and Vineyardist, David's son, Peter, is now Assistant Winemaker. Walter's son, Steve, is Assistant Vineyardist. The vineyard is located at the winery. Ficklin specializes in one wine—Tinta Port.

FIELDBROOK VALLEY WINERY
Fieldbrook Road, Fieldbrook, CA 95521
Founded 1976. The Owner and Winemaker is Robert Hodgson. The varietal wine produced is Riesling.

FIELD STONE WINERY
10075 Highway 128, Healdsburg, CA 95448
Sonoma County
Storage: American, French and German oak, st. steel
Founded 1966. The Owner is Mrs. Marion Johnson. The Winemaker is Deborah Ann Cutter. The vineyard is located at the winery in the Alexander Valley. The Estate-bottled, 100% varietal wines produced are: Johannisberg Riesling (Late Harvest), Chenin Blanc, Gewurztraminer, Cabernet Sauvignon, Petite Sirah, Rosé Of Petite Sirah, and Spring-Cabernet (White wine, not a Rosé).

The Winemaker's favorite wines are: Spring Cabernet, Petite Sirah Rosé, Cabernet Sauvignon and Petite Sirah.

FILIPPI VINTAGE CO.
Box 2, Mira Loma, CA 91752
San Bernardino County
Storage: Oak, redwood and st. steel
Founded 1934. The Owners are The Filippi Family. The Winemaker is Joseph A. Filippi. The family has been making wine for generations. Wine is sold direct to the consumer through sales and tasting rooms.

Fine

Fining, the process of clearing young wines by adding beaten egg, lactic acid, heavy gelatin, etc.

Finish

The very last impression of the tasting mouthful.

Fino

Denoting the qualities of dryness and lightness in Sherry.

FIRESTONE VINEYARD

P.O. Box 244, Los Olivos, CA 93441

Santa Barbara County

Founded 1974. The Owner is Brooks Firestone. The Winemaker is Anthony Austin. The vineyards are located at the winery in the Santa Ynez Valley. Vintage-dated, varietal wines produced are: Gewurztraminer, Chardonnay, Rosé of Cabernet, Sauvignon Blanc, Cabernet Sauvignon, Pinot Noir, Johannisberg Riesling and Merlot.

Special harvest varietals, vintage-dated are: Gewurztraminer and Johannisberg Riesling.

Also produced are: "Red Wine," "White Wine" and non-vintage Cabernet Sauvignon. The Winemaker's favorite wine is Pinot Noir (Vintage Reserve).

FIRPO WINERY

Route 2, Oakley, CA 94561

Contra Costa County

FISHER VINEYARDS

6200 St. Helena Road, Santa Rosa, CA 95404

Sonoma County

Storage: French and German oak, st. steel

Owners are Fred J. Fisher and Juelle L. Fisher. Winemaster is Charles Ortman. Winemaker is Fred Fisher; Vineyards are located in Napa Valley; Sonoma County. Varietal wines produced are Cabernet Sauvignon and Chardonnay.

FITCH MOUNTAIN VINEYARDS

(See Richert & Sons Winery)

Flinty

Often used to describe wine that is dry, clean, sharp.

Flor

A selected yeast culture which, under suitable conditions, grows on the surface of wine and produces the flavor characteristic in Sherries, so named.

FLORA SPRINGS WINE CO.

1885 W. Zinfandel Lane, St. Helena, CA 94574

Napa County

Storage: American and French oak, st. steel.

The Owners are John and Carrie Komes, Julie and Pat Garvey and S.A. Cisler. The Winemakers are Ken Deis and S. A. Cisler. The vineyards are located in Napa.

Varietal, vintage-dated, Estate-bottled wines produced are: Cabernet Sauvignon, Chardonnay, Sauvignon Blanc and Riesling.

Folle Blanche

(White Table Wine) A varietal grape that produces a dry, tart, fruity and fresh tasting wine with a mild aroma that is both apple and grapey. Goes well with fish, poultry and casseroles.

Originally from France where it once was the Cognac grape. Produced in California only by Louis Martini.

FOPPIANO VINEYARDS

Box 606, Healdsburg, CA 95448

Sonoma County

Storage: Oak, redwood, st. steel.

Founded 1896. Owned, operated and managed by the Foppiano Family. The President is Louis J., grandson of John, who founded the vineyard, in 1896. Louis M. is the Manager and the Winemaker is Rod. The vineyards are along the Russian River.

Under the Louis J. Foppiano label the varietal, vintage-dated wines are: Sonoma Fumé (100%), Chenin Blanc (100%), Russian River Valley Chardonnay (100%), Russian River Valley, Dry French Colombard, Dry Chenin Blanc, Pinot Chardonnay, Russian River Valley Pinot Noir, Sonoma County Zinfandel (100%), Russian River Valley Petite Sirah (100%) and Sonoma County Cabernet Sauvignon.

Also produced are: vintage-dated Sonoma County, Sonoma White Burgundy, Sweet French Colombard and Sweet Chenin Blanc.

Under the Foppiano label, these jug wines are produced: Chablis, Zinfandel, Burgundy and Vin Rosé.

The Winemaker's favorite wines are: Petite Sirah and Sonoma Fumé.

FORMAN WINERY

2555 Madrona Ave., St. Helena, CA 94574

Napa County

Storage: French oak barrels and st. steel

Owners, P. L. Newton and R. W. Forman; The Winemaker is R. W. Forman. Wines produced are Red (Blend of Cabarnet Sauvignon, Merlot and Cabernet Franc), White (Blend of Sauvignon Blanc and Semillion). Vineyards, 50 acres.

FORTINO WINERY

4525 Hecker Pass Highway, Gilroy, CA 95020

Santa Clara County

Storage: Oak and redwood.

The Owners are Ernest and Marie Fortino. Ernest is the Winemaker. The vineyard is located at the winery. As of 1980, in the first 10 years since the winery was founded, it had won 32 medals in tasting competitions.

The varietal wines produced are: Zinfandel "Blanc," Cabernet Sauvignon "Blanc," Johannisberg Riesling, Carignane, Zinfandel, Ruby Cabernet, Petite Sirah, Charbono, Cabernet Sauvignon, Grenache Ruby, Rosé Of Cabernet Sauvignon and Zinfandel Rosé. The other wines produced are: Chablis, Haut Sauterne, Vin Rosé Reserve, Chianti and Burgundy Reserve.

Foxiness

An unpleasant characteristic of some native Eastern American grape species—the Vitis Labrusca.

FRANCISCAN VINEYARDS

1678 Galleron Road, Rutherford, CA 94573
Napa County
The Owner is the Peter Eckes Co. Justin Meyer is President and Winemaker of Franciscan. The vineyards are in the Napa Valley, Napa County and Alexander Valley, Sonoma County.

The varietal, vintage-dated wines produced are: Napa Valley Cabernet Sauvinon, Alexander Valley Cabernet Sauvignon, Private Reserve Cabernet Sauvignon, Sonoma County Cabernet Sauvignon, Napa Valley Charbono, Napa Valley Chardonnay, Temecula Chardonnay, Napa Valley White Riesling, Napa Valley Pinot Noir Blanc, California Fumé Blanc, Temecula Johannisberg Riesling, California Chenin Blanc, Lake County Gamay Rosé and Muscat Del Sol.

Also produced are: California Burgundy and Chablis.

The Winemaker's favorite wines are: Cabernet Sauvignon (Napa Valley and Alexander Valley), Napa Valley White Riesling and Napa Valley Chardonnay.

FRASINETTI WINERY

7395 Frasinetti Road, Sacramento, CA
Sacramento County
Owners are Howard and Gary Frasinetti. The grapes are purchased on a selected district basis. This is the oldest family winery in Sacramento, started in 1897 by James Frasinetti.

Franken Riesling

Not a true Riesling. (See Sylvaner)

FRANZIA WINERY

1700 E. Hwy. 120, Ripon, CA 95366
San Joaquin County
Storage: st. steel
The Owner is the Coca Cola Bottling Co. of New York. The Winemaker is Jim Wells. The vineyards are located in the San Joaquin Valley.

Varietal wines produced are Zinfandel, Chenin Blanc, French Colombard, Cabernet Sauvignon and Grenache Rosé.

Also produced are Chablis, Rhine, Rhinefluer, Golden Chablis, Pink Chablis, Vin Rosé, Burgundy, Burgundy Noir, White and Red Port, Muscatel, Sherry, Spumonte, Ruby Chablis, Sparkling Burgundy, Sparkling Rosé, Champagne and Pink Champagne.

French Colombard

The second most widely planted white wine grape in California, (after Thompson Seedless). It is grown in virtually all areas and is most prolific in the San Joaquin Valley where it is relied on heavily to provide acid for blending the dry white wines, for distillation into Brandy, and Champagne production. It is the more reliable of the dry white jug wines and still a good value. Look for these French Colombards: Beringer Los Hermanos, Barengo, Chalone, Gavilan, E & J Gallo, Giumarra, Parducci, Inglenook, Italian Swiss Colony, Sonoma Vineyards, Souverain, Richard Carey.

FREEMARK ABBEY WINERY

3022 St. Helena Hwy North, St. Helena, CA 94574
Napa County
Storage: French oak and st. steel
The winery is owned by a limited partnership. The Wine-
maker is Larry Langbehn. Winemaking at the Freemark
Abbey dates back to 1886. The vineyards are located in
the Napa Valley. Grapes are also purchased on a select
vineyard basis.
Varietal, vintage dated wines produced are Chardonnay,
Johannisberg Riesling, Edelwein (Sweet Johannisberg
Riesling), Pinot Noir, Cabernet Sauvignon and Petite
Sirah.

FRESNO COUNTY

(Central San Joaquin Valley) B. Cribari & Sons (Guild),
Gibson Winery, E & J Gallo, Villa Bianchi, A. Nonini
Winery, Farnesi Winery, Landis Vineyard.

FRESNO, KERN, MADERA, MERCED, TULARE

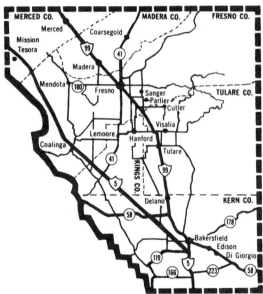

FRETTER WINE CELLARS

805 Camelia Street, Berkeley, CA 94710
Alameda County
Owner and Winemaker is William Fretter. Grapes are
purchased on a select vineyard basis from Napa, Sonoma
and Mendocino.
Varietal wines produced are Chardonnay, Cabernet
Sauvignon, Pinot Noir, Gamay, Gamay Rose, Merlot and
Semillon.

FRICK WINERY

303 Potrero St., Santa Cruz, CA 95060

Santa Cruz County

The Owners and Winemakers are Bill and Judith Frick. Grapes are purchased on a select vineyard basis.

100% varietal, vintage-dated wines produced are Pinot Noir, Chardonnay, Petite Sirah, Zinfandel and Chenin Blanc.

The Winemaker's favorite wines are Pinot Noir, Petite Sirah and Chardonnay.

Fume Blanc

(See Sauvignon Blanc) This term has become more popular to describe this increasingly consumed dry, crisp white wine.

G

GALLEANO WINERY

4231 Wineville Road, Mira Loma, CA 91752

Riverside County

Storage: Oak, redwood and concrete.

Founded 1933. The Owner is the Galleano Family. B. D. Galleano is the Winemaker. The vineyard dates back eighty years to General Cantu, former Governor of Baja, California. Domenico Galleano purchased the vineyard in 1918. The vineyard is in the Cucamonga district.

Wines produced are both generic and varietal. Galleano wines are not sold out of the State.

The Winemaker's favorite is Zinfandel.

THE WINE CELLARS OF ERNEST AND JULIO GALLO

P.O. Box 1130, Modesto, CA 95353

Stanislaus County

The Owners are Ernest and Julio Gallo. The Winemaker is Julio Gallo. The Gallos began in 1933, have been, and continue to be, the pace and trend-setters in the California wine industry. They are the largest wine producers in the world, with the kind of demand for quality that is sought and desired by a great classic Chateau. They are on a constant search for viticultural improvement— the art of creating varietal and generic wines of the highest quality still has the personal attention of Ernest and Julio and their immediate family. The Gallo vineyards are located in Mendocino, Sonoma, Napa, Lodi, Monterey, Modesto, Livingston and Fresno.

Under the label "The Wine Cellars of Ernest and Julio Gallo" the varietal wines produced are: Sauvignon Blanc, Chenin Blanc, Johannisberg Riesling, Gewurztraminer, French Colombard, Zinfandel and Barbera. Also produced is Rosé.

Under the "Gallo" label the wines produced are: Burgundy, Hearty Burgundy, Rhine, Chablis Blanc, Pink Chablis, Red Rosé, Vin Rosé and Chianti of California. Also California Champagne.

GAMBARELLI AND DAVITTO
(See United Vintners)

Gamay
(Red Table Wine) A varietal light, fruity, fresh and slightly tart wine. Originally from the Burgundy region of France where it is the dominant grape in Beaujolais. Also referred to as *Napa Gamay*. Should be drunk when still young—one or two years old. Some enjoy this red wine slightly chilled. Look for: Almaden, Chappellet, J. Lohr, Mill Creek, Robert Mondavi, Ridge, Raymond, San Pasqual and Trentadue, Geyser Peak.

Gamay Beaujolais
(Red Table Wine) A varietal grape that produces a light, fresh wine very much in the style of Gamay. The Gamay Beaujolais is a sub-variety of Pinot Noir. Look for: Durney, Jekel, Monterey Vineyards, Charles Krug, Robert Pecota, Parducci, Paul Masson, Stags Leap Wine Cellars, Sebastiani, Sterling, Weibel, Beringer.

Gamay Noir
(Red Table Wine) A red varietal wine made from the Gamay.

GamayRosé
(Pink Table Wine) A varietal pink table wine that is fresh, fruity and slightly sweet, made from the Gamay. Look for: Chappellet, Robert Mondavi, Charles Krug, Almaden, Barengo, Paul Masson, Geyser Peak.

GAUTHIER & CLEVENGE LTD.
(See Vikings Four)

PAUL GARRETTS VINTNERS CHOICE
(See Guild Wineries)

GAVILAN
(See Chalone Vineyard)

GEMELLO WINERY
2003 El Camino Real, Mountain View, CA 94040
Santa Clara County
Storage: Oak, redwood, st. steel.
Founded 1934. The Owners are the Gemello Family. The Winemaker is Mario J. Gemello. Varietal wines produced are: Petite Sirah, Cabernet Sauvignon (Santa Clara), Pinot Noir (Sonoma County), Barbera, Chardonnay and Chenin Blanc. Winemakers favorites are Cabernet Sauvignon and Zinfandel.

Generic
Wine-type names which stand for definite type characteristics are called "generic" or "semi-generic"—generic names of geographic origin originally applied to the wines of specific Old World vitacultural districts; as those wines became famous, their names, through the centuries, came to designate any wines with similar characteristics, wherever grown. Burgundy, Champagne, Claret, Port, Rhine Wine, Sauterne and Sherry are the best-known semi-generic wine-type names of geographic origin. Vermouth is a generic name without geographic significance.

Gewurztraminer
(White Table Wine) A varietal grape that produces an

aromatic, medium-bodied, spicy-in-character wine with the slightest touch of sweetness. In German, "gewurz" means spicy—and that actually describes the wine. It has an unique floral spiciness like that of carnation—rather than that of cinnamon or ginger. Mostly preferred before dinner with appetizers. It also goes well with salmon, pork, poultry and sausages. Serve chilled. There are a few produced dry in the "Alsace" style. Look for Almaden, Buena Vista, Chateau St. Jean, Richard Carey (Late Harvest), Clos du Bois, Christian Brothers (Dry), Dry Creek "Late Harvest", Edmeades, Firestone, "Select Late Harvest", Firestone, Gundlach-Bundschu, Gallo, Geyser Peak, Grand Cru, Hacienda, Hop Kiln, Husch, Heitz, Inglenook, Mark West, Monterey Vineyard, Mirassou (Dry), Matanzas, Louis M. Martini (Dry), Joseph Phelps, Pedroncelli, Simi, Stony Hill (Dry), Villa Mt. Eden (Dry), Wente, Z-D (Dry).

GEYSER PEAK WINERY
12281 Redwood Hwy, Geyserville, CA 95441
Sonoma County
Storage: Oak, redwood and st. steel.
The Owner is the Joseph Schlitz Brewing Company. The Winemaker is Armand Bussone. The winery was originally founded in 1880. The vineyards are located in Sonoma County.

Varietal, vintage-dated wines produced are: Cabernet Sauvignon, Chardonnay, Chenin Blanc, Johannisberg Riesling, Fumé Blanc, Gewurztraminer, Pinot Noir, Pinot Noir Blanc, Zinfandel and Rosé Cabernet Sauvignon.

Also produced are vintage-dated Chablis and Burgundy.

Also Brut California Champagne.

GIBSON WINE CO.
1720 Academy St., Sanger, CA 93657
Fresno County
Second Winery:
9750 Kent Street, Elk Grove, Sacramento, CA 95624
Sacramento County
Founded 1934. Gibson is owned by about 150 growers who are members of a Cooperative. Alex Farafontoff is the Winemaker in Elk Grove, Gerald D. Homulka in Sanger. The vineyards are in Fresno, Tulare and Kings Counties.

The wines produced under the Gibson Vineyards label are: Chablis, Rhine, Vin Rosé, Burgundy, Chianti, Chablis Blanc, Sauterne, Pink Chablis, Vino Pastoso and Vino Rosso. Also produced as "Premium Select" are Sherry, Port, Muscatel, Tokay and Muscatel.

Under the Oregon label Retsina and Kokinelli Greek-style wines are produced.

The Winemaker's favorite wine is Chablis.

GIRETTI WINERY
791-5th Street, Gilroy, CA 95020
Santa Clara County
Owners, Peter and Harry Giretti.

GIUMARRA VINEYARDS

Edison Road and Edison Highway, Edison, CA 93303
Kern County
Storage: st. steel
The Owners are The Giumarra Family. Joe Giumarra is
Chairman of the Board and Sal is President. The Wine-
makers are Dale Anderson and Bill Nakata. Three gen-
erations oversee the winery and vineyards. It all started
with "Papa" Joe when he bought his first land in the San
Joaquin Valley, in 1922. The vineyards are in Kern
County and other districts.

The varietal wines produced are: Cabernet Sauvignon,
Gamay Beaujolais, Petite Sirah, Zinfandel, Barbera,
Ruby Cabernet, Pinot Noir, Napa Gamay, Carnelian,
Emerald Riesling, Chenin Blanc, French Colombard,
Semillon, Green Hungarian, Chardonnay, Napa Gamay
Rosé, Gamay Beaujolais Rosé, Carnelian Rosé and Ca-
bernet Sauvignon Rosé. Also produced are: Burgundy,
Dry Red, Royalty, Rubired, Vino Rosso, Chablis, Dry
White, Sauterne, Pink Chablis, Vin Rosé, White Port,
Angelica, Sherry, Muscatel, Port, Tokay Light Sweet
White, Red and Muscat.

GLEN OAK HILLS WINERY

40607 Los Ranchos Circle, Temecula, CA 92390
Riverside County
Storage: Oak barrels and st. steel.
Owner and Winemaker is Hugo Woerdemann. The
grapes are purchased on a selected vineyard *district* ba-
sis.

Varietal wines produced are: Cabernet Sauvignon,
Zinfandel, Chardonnay, Sauvignon Blanc, Chenin Blanc
and White Riesling.

GOLD BELL

(See East-Side Winery)

GOLD NUGGETT

(See Amador Winery)

GOLDEN BONANZA

(See Yankee Hill Winery)

GOLD MINE

(See California Cellarmasters)

GRAND CRU VINEYARDS

#1 Vintage Lane, Glen Ellen, CA 95442
Sonoma County
Storage: Oak, redwood and st. steel.
The Owners are Allen Ferrera and Robert Magnani. Rob-
ert is the Winemaker. The vineyards are located at the
winery. Wines produced are: 100% varietal Chenin
Blanc, Pinot Noir Blanc, Gewurztraminer, Cabernet
Sauvignon, Zinfandel and "Induced Botrytis" Gewurz-
traminer.

GRAND PACIFIC VINEYARD

134 Paul Drive, #9, San Rafael, CA 94901
Marin County
Storage: Oak barrels and st. steel.
The Owner and Winemaker is Richard B. Dye. The
grapes are purchased on a selected district vineyard ba-
sis.   *(continued)*

Varietal wines produced are: Cabernet Sauvignon, Merlot, Chardonnay and White Riesling.

GRAN VAL
(See Clos Du Val)

GRAVELLY MEADOW
(See Diamond Creek Vineyards)

Green
Disagreeable acidity—usually in young wine.

Green Hungarian
(White Table Wine) A varietal grape that produces a light, neutral fresh and semi-dry wine; drink young. Look for: Buena Vista, Sebastiani, Weibel.

GREEN & RED VINEYARD
3208 Chiles Pope Valley Road, St. Helena, CA 94574
Napa County
Storage: Oak and st. steel
Founded 1977. Owner and Winemaker, Jay Heminway.
Vineyard is at Chiles Canyon hillside, Napa Valley. The varietal vintage dated wine produced is Zinfandel.

ANNIE GREEN SPRINGS
(See United Vintners)

GREEN VALLEY
(See Galleano Winery)

GREENWOOD RIDGE VINEYARD
1090 Greenwood Ridge, Philo, CA 95466
Mendocino County

Grenache
(Red Table Wine) A varietal grape that is predominantly used for Rosé because of its pale color and strong flavor.

Grenache Rosé
(Pink Table Wine) A varietal grape that is mainly used for Rosé. When used for Rosé, the grapes' strong character is much tempered. A fruity, light, tart wine that has a noticeable sweetness. Originally from the Tavel region of France. Serve with ham, turkey, picnics and luncheon. Look for: Almaden, Gallo, Sonoma Vineyards, Cresta Blanca, Live Oaks, Franzia.

Grey Riesling
(White Table Wine) A varietal grape that produces a light, fresh, slightly-sweet, but delicate, wine. Originally from France under the name Chauché gris. Serves well with poultry, fish and picnics. Look for: Wente Bros. who have pioneered this variety and made it very popular.

Greystone
(See Perelli-Minetti Winery) Also used by insiders at Christian Bros. to describe the historic old stone winery in St. Helena

GRGICH HILLS CELLAR
1829 St. Helena Highway, Rutherford, CA 94573
Napa County
Storage: French oak
The Owners are Miljenko (Mike) Grgich and Austin Mills. The Winemaker is Miljonko (Mike) Grgich, formerly of Chateau Montelena where he created the Char-

donnay which stormed Paris in 1976. The vineyards are in Rutherford and Napa, all Napa Valley.

Varietal, vintage-dated wines produced are: Late Harvest Napa Valley Johannisberg Riesling, Napa Valley Johannisberg Riesling, Sonoma Zinfandel and Napa Valley Chardonnay.

GRIFFIN VINEYARD
(See Hop Kiln Winery)

Grignolino
(Red Table Wine) A varietal grape that produces a tart, sharp wine with an orange pigment character. Should be drunk two to five years old. Originally from Northern Italy. Excellent with rich meat dishes. Look for: Heitz, San Martin, Beringer and Cadenasso. A relatively rare variety, something of a curiosity.

GROVER GULCH WINERY
7880 Glen Haven Road, Soquel, CA 95073
Santa Cruz County
Storage: Oak barrels
The Owners and Winemakers are Dennis Bassano and Reinhold Banek. The grapes are purchased on a select region basis.

Varietal wines produced are: Cabernet Sauvignon, Carignane, Grenache and Petit Sirah.

GROWERS
(See California Growers Winery)

GUASTI
(See Perelli-Minetti)

EMILIO GUGLIELMO WINERY
1480 East Main Ave., Morgan Hill, CA 95037
Santa Clara County
Storage: Oak and redwood.
The Owner is the George W. Guglielmo Family. The Winemaker is George E. Guglielmo. Founded by Emilio, owned by his son, George, and operated by his grandsons, George E. and Eugene. The vineyard is located at the winery in the Santa Clara Valley.

Under the Emilielmo label the varietal, vintage-dated Estate-bottled wines produced are: Semillon Blanc, Sylvaner Riesling, Johannisberg Riesling (100%), Grignolino Rosé (100%), Gamay Rosé (100%), Gamay Beaujolais (100%), Zinfandel (95%), Barbera (100%), Ruby Cabernet, Petite Sirah (98%), Cabernet Sauvignon (100%) and Zinfandel (100%). Also produced are Chablis Blanc and Burgundy.

Under the Emile's label the premium jug wines produced are: Chablis, Blanc Sec, Vin Rosé, Mellow Burgundy, Grignolino Rosé (100%), Chenin Blanc (100%) and Santa Clara Valley Burgundy. (These are a good value when you can find them.) Also produced are Champagne, Sherry and Port.

GUILD WINERIES
500 Sansome St., San Francisco, CA 94111
Wineries in Fresno, Lodi, Woodbridge, Del Rio, Delano, Sanger and Ukiah. Tasting Rooms: Lodi and Fresno. The

Owner is the Guild Corporation. The President is Robert M. Ivie. The Winemaker is Albert B. Cribari. The wineries produce Cresta Blanca in Ukiah, Mendocino County and Cribari in Fresno. Other Guild labels are: Guild Vino da Tavola, Paul Garrett Vintners Choice, Roma, Roma di California, Roma diUva and Winemasters.

Varietal wines produced under the Cresta Blanca label are: Grenache Rosé, Pinot Chardonnay, Gewurztraminer, Chenin Blanc and/or Santa Barbara Chenin Blanc, Johannisberg Riesling, Mendocino French Colombard, Cabernet Sauvignon, Pinot Noir, Mendocino Zinfandel, Petite Sirah, Mendocino Gamay Beaujolais and Carnelian.

Also produced are: Chablis and/or Mendocino Chablis, North Coast and/or Mendocino Burgundy and Blanc de Blanc.

Under the Winemasters label the wines produced are Mountain Burgundy, Mountain Nectar Vin Rosé, Rhine, Mountain White Chablis, Chianti, Sauterne and Pink Chablis.

Under the Winemasters label the varietal wines produced are. Zinfandel Cabernet Sauvignon, Chenin Blanc, French Colombard, Green Hungarian, Grenache Rosé, Johannisberg Riesling, Petite Sirah, Pinot Noir and White Burgundy.

Under the Cribari California Wines label are produced: Vino Rosso, Vino Bianco, Vino Fiamma, Vino Chianti, Mountain Chablis, Vin Rosé, Mellow Burgundy, Rhine, Sauterne, Pink Chablis, Extra Dry Chablis and Mendocino Burgundy.

Varietals produced are: Grenache Rosé, Zinfandel, Barbera, Cabernet Sauvignon and Pinot Chardonnay.

They also own Cresta Blanca Winery in Ukiah. They produce a number of good brandies, Ceremony, Directors Choice, Guild and St. Mark. Also a very unique product: Silverado Vodka, the only one made 100% from grapes.

GUNDLACH-BUNDSCHU WINERY
3775 Thornberry Road, Sonoma, CA 95487
Sonoma County
Storage: Oak barrels and st. steel.
Founded 1858. Owners are James T. Bundschu and John and Susan Merritt, Jr. The Winemaker is John Merritt, Jr. Founded in 1858 by Jacob Gundlach, a few years later its name was changed to its current one when Jame's great-grandfather became a Partner in the business. The winery still maintains its original Bonded Winery Number 64 from the United States Government. The vineyards are located in the Sonoma Valley.

Varietal, vintage-dated, Estate-bottled wines produced are: Sonoma Valley Cabernet Sauvignon and Sonoma Valley Zinfandel.

Varietal, vintage-dated wines produced are: Late Harvest, Mendocino Johannisberg Riesling, Johannisberg Riesling, Gewurztraminer, Sonoma Riesling and Sonoma County Chardonnay. *(continued)*

Also produced is Estate-bottled and vintage-dated Sonoma Valley Kleinberger (White wine).

The Winemaker's favorite is Cabrenet Sauvignon and Gewurztraminer.

H

HACIENDA WINE CELLARS

1000 Vineyard Ave., Sonoma, CA 95476

Sonoma County

Storage: Oak, redwood and st. steel.

Founded 1973. The Owners are F. H. Bartholomew and A. Crawford Coolley. Bartholomew owned Buena Vista for years. The Winemaker is Steven W. MacRostie. Hacienda is located in the midst of the historic Buena Vista Vineyard originally founded by Agoston Haraszthy in 1862. Vineyard was purchased by F. H. Bartholomew in 1941.

Varietal, vintage-dated wines produced are Chardonnay (100%), Cabernet Sauvignon (100%), Gewurztraminer (100%), Chenin Blanc, Johannisberg Riesling, Pinot Noir-Blanc, Zinfandel and Pinot Noir.

The Winemaker's favorite wines are Cabernet Sauvignon and Gewurztraminer.

HALE CELLARS

P. O. Box 5, Los Alamos, CA 93440

Owners, Sam and Dona Hale.

HARASZTHY CELLARS

(See Buena Vista Winery)

J. J. HARASZTHY & SON

14301 Arnold Drive, Glen Ellen, CA 95442

Sonoma County

Storage: st. steel.

Founded 1978. Owners, Jan and Vallejo Haraszthy. Val is the winemaker. Vinyard is in Sonoma County. Varietal wines produced are Zinfandel, Gewurztraminer, Johannisberg Riesling and Pinot Noir.

HANZELL VINEYARDS

18596 Lomita Ave., Sonoma, CA 95476

SonomaCounty

Storage: French oak and st. steel.

Founded 1976. The Owner is Mrs. Barbara de Crye. The Winemaker is Robert Sessions. The vineyards are located at the winery in Sonoma Valley- It was founded by the late Ambassador Zellerbach.

Varietal, vintage-dated, Estate-bottled wines produced are: Pinot Noir and Chardonnay, in the tradition of the great Burgundian winemakers. (34 acres only 5,600 gallons per year.)

HARBOR WINERY

610 Harbor Blvd., West Sacramento, CA 95831

Yolo County

Storage: Oak and st. steel.

Owners and Winemaker, Charles H. Myers. *(continued)*

Wines produced are Cabernet Sauvignon, Chardonnay and Mission del Sol.

HAVELOCK GORDON NEGOCIANTS

Stanford Wine Co.

P.O. Box 1080, Palo Alto, CA 94302

Bonsal Seggerman & Co.

27 The Plaza, Locust Valley, NY 11560

Havelock Gordon Negociants program is very much like the traditional Burgundian Negociant. Paul Draper Selection is indicated. Regularly offered are Chardonnay, Cabernet Sauvignon and Zinfandel. Occasionally other varietals and generics.

HAWK CREST

(See Stag's Leap Wine Cellars)

Heat, Heat Summation "Regions"

The classifying of areas according to their ability to grow certain varieties of wine grapes. Rainfall, humidity, latitude, soil types, etc. are not considered.

The basic theory is that grape vines do not show a net positive metabolism until the temperature around the vine reaches 50° F. Below 50° F, nothing happens that will produce or ripen grapes. The vine remains passive. Above 50° F, the vine shows a net gain and it uses this energy (sugar) to develop and ripen its grapes. You can add up the "usuable sun's heat" for a season in any vineyard by recording each day's high and low, then calculating the median temperature in that vineyard. For example, a summer day in which the average temperature was 80° F. is a day which average temperature was 30° above the 50° base and it would, therefore, contribute 30 degree-days to the total heat summation that the vineyard will receive during the season. The world's wine-growing regions are classified as: Region I: up to 2,500 degree-days; Region II: 2,501–3,000 degree-days; Region III: 3,001–3,500 degree-days; Region IV: 3,501–4,000 degree-days; Region V: above 4,000 degree days. Generally speaking, the best-known and highest quality areas for table wines are cool and fall into Regions I or II (sometimes a low III). If the temperature is high, the vine produces sugar faster than if the temperature is low. The problem is that grapes grown in warm climates have less flavor than if the same grapes were grown in cooler climates.

HECKER PASS WINERY

4605 Hecker Pass Highway, Gilroy, CA 95020

Santa Clara County

Storage: Oak and redwood.

Founded 1972. The Owner and Winemaker is Mario Fortino. The vineyard is located at the winery.

The varietal wines produced are: Ruby Cabernet, Carignane, Zinfandel, Petite Sirah and Chenin Blanc. Other wines produced are Chablis, Vin Rosé, Vino Rosso, Petite Sirah Select, Grenache Nouveau, Cream Sherry, Medium Dry Sherry and Port.

HEITZ WINE CELLARS

500 Taplin Road, St. Helena, CA 94574   *(continued)*

Napa County

Storage: Oak, redwood and st. steel.

Founded 1961. The Owner is the Heitz Family. The Winemakers are Joseph E. and Son, David T. Heitz. Grapes are purchased on a select vineyard basis. The most famous Heitz wine is the Martha's Vineyard Cabernet Sauvignon, which comes from Tom & Martha May's Vineyard near Oakville.

Varietal, vintage-dated wines produced are: Napa Valley, Cabernet Sauvignon, Martha's Vineyard Cabernet Sauvignon, Fay Vineyard Cabernet Sauvignon, Grignolino Rosé, Napa Valley Pinot Chardonnay, Sweet Johannisberg Riesling, Johannisberg Riesling and Gewurztraminer.

Also produced are: Grignolino, Barbera, Burgundy, Chablis, Champagne, "Cellar Treasure" Sherry, Port and Angelica.

The Winemaker's favorite wines are Cabernet Sauvignon (Fay Vineyards) and Pinot Chardonnay.

HERRERA VINEYARDS

17177 Bodega Highway, Bodega, CA 94922
Sonoma County

WILLIAM HILL WINERY

P.O. Box 3989, Napa, CA 94558
Napa County

Founded 1976. The Owner and Winemaker is William Hill; Vineyard, 285 acres. The vineyards are located at the winery in Napa.

Varietal, vintage-dated, Estate-bottled wines produced are: Cabernet Sauvignon and Chardonnay.

History of Early California

The Jesuit Fathers carried Spanish colonization and wine-growing up the Western Coast into the Mexican Peninsula of Baja, California. Their successors, the Franciscans, advanced into what is now the State of California. As each new settlement or mission was established, vines were planted as one of the first steps in transforming wilderness into civilization.

The Franciscans and their leader, Padré Junipero Serra, established Mission San Diego, in 1769, and planted wine grapes there. Thus, it was discovered that California was a land especially favored for wine-growing. In Northern Mexico and Baja, California these pioneers of western wine-growing suffered many hardships in cultivating the arrid lands and in trying to supply themselves with wines needed for sacramental and table use. At San Diego, the grapevines thrived and the wines were better.

As the Franciscans moved northward, establishing new missions, they found the same results. They had discovered a new wine-growing region. More than a century later, it was destined to become one of the premier wine regions of the world.

Eventually, Padré Serra's missionairies built a chain of 21 missions, from San Diego to Sonoma. Sonoma was the northernmost point of their El Camino Real or

"Kings Highway." They planted vineyards and made wine at nearly all of the missions. San Gabriel Mission, near Los Angeles, was the site of their largest winery. There they had three wine presses. Mission San Diego and its vineyards were established six years before the American Revolution.

H. M. S. FROST

(See United Vintners)

Hock

A dry, white table wine usually made with Riesling grapes, in which, as with other white wines, the fermentation takes place after the skins have been separated. Hock was originally produced in Hockiem, Germany.

HMR (HOFFMAN MOUNTAIN RANCH) VINEYARDS

Adelaida Road, Star Route, Paso Robles, CA 93446
San Luis Obispo County

Founded 1972. Owned by the Hoffman Family and operated by Dr. Stanley Hoffman and sons, David and Michael. Michael is the Winemaker. The Vineyards are in the foothills of Santa Lucia mountains near Paso Robles. The winery has won many medals in various categories. The 100% Estate-bottled varietal wines produced are: Zinfandel, Chardonnay, Johannisberg Riesling, Franken Riesling, Chenin Blanc, Grenache Rosé, Cabernet Sauvignon and Pinot Noir.

The Winemaker's favorites are the Rieslings, Chardonnay and Pinot Noir.

HOP KILN WINERY AT GRIFFIN VINEYARD

6050 Westside Road, Healdsburg, CA 95448
Sonoma County

Storage: Oak and st. steel.

Founded 1975. The Owner and Winemaker is L. Martin Griffin, M.D. The vineyards are located at the winery. Because of age, being planted in 1880 and having been in continuous production, the winery and vineyard have been designated a California Historical Landmark. The name derives from the Hop drying barns on the property as this was previously a prime hop growing area. The winery has won many medals in competitive wine tastings.

The 100% varietal, Estate-bottled wines produced are: French Colombard, Gewurztraminer, Gamay Beaujolais and Petite Sirah. Also produced is "Late Harvest" Johannisberg Riesling, Zinfandel, "Weihnachten" Johannisberg Riesling (Late Select Botrytis) and A Thousand Flowers (Dry White Table Wine) blend of Johannisberg Riesling, French Colombard and Gewurztraminer.

The Winemaker's favorite wines are "A Thousand Flowers" and Gewurztraminer.

HORIZON WINERY

2594 Athena Court, Santa Rosa, CA 95401
Sonoma County

Storage: Oak.

Founded 1977. Owner and Winemaker, Paul D. Gardner; vineyard is in Sonoma County. Varietal wines produced are Zinfandel and Petite Sirah.

HUGO'S CELLAR
(See Glenoak Hills Winery)

HULTGREN & SAMPERTON
2201 Westside Road, Healdsburg, CA 95448
Sonoma County
Storage: French oak.
Owners, Edward Samperton and J. Leonard Hultgren;
Winemaker, Edward Samperton; Vineyards are in Dry
Creek Valley and Alexander Valley. Varietal wines pro-
duced are Cabernet Sauvignon, Chardonnay, Pinot Noir
and Gamay Beaujolais.

HUMBOLDT COUNTY
(Northernmost Coastal) Willow Creek Vineyards, Witt-
ner Winery

HUSCH VINEYARDS
4900 Star Route, Philo, CA 95466
Mendocino County
Storage: Oak and st. steel.
Founded 1978 by Tony and Gretchen Husch. The Owner
is Hugo A. Oswald; the Winemaker is Alfred White; the
Vineyard is in the Anderson Valley.
    Varietal, vintage-dated wines produced are: Pinot
Noir, Pinot Noir Rosé, Cabernet Sauvignon, Chardonnay,
Gewurztraminer and Johannisberg Riesling.

I

INDIAN CREEK
(See Navarro Vineyards)

INGLENOOK VINEYARDS
P.O. Box 19, Rutherford, CA 94573
Napa County
Founded 1879 by Capt. Neibaum. The Owner is the Heu-
blein Company (United Vintners). Vice President and
General Manager of Inglenook is Robert Furek. The
Winemaker is Thomas Ferrell. The vineyards are in
three wine growing areas and are labeled as such.
    Varietal, vintage-dated, Estate-bottled and Cask Lim-
ited wines are Chenin Blanc, Cabernet Sauvignon, Fumé
Blanc, Blanc de Noir, Muscat Blanc, Charbono, Zinfan-
del, Petite Sirah, Pinot Chardonnay, Gewurztrainer, Jo-
hannisberg Riesling, Pinot St. George, Pinot Noir, Gamay Beaujolais and Gamay Rosé. The grapes for these
wines all come from the Napa Valley. The Vintage line
of wines produced from grapes grown in the North Coast
Counties and all carrying a vintage date are Burgundy,
Chablis, Rhine and Cabernet Rosé.
The Navalle line of wines are produced from California
grapes; the wines are Zinfandel, Chablis, Burgundy,
Rhine, Vin Rosé, Riesling, French Colombard, Chenin
Blanc, and Ruby Cabernet.
    Inglenook also produces Medium Dry, Pale Dry and
Cream Sherry, Tawny and Ruby Port. Recommend: Char-
bono and Blanc de Noir.

IRON HORSE VINEYARDS
9786 Ross Station Road, Sebastopol, CA 95472

Sonoma County
Storage: Oak and st. steel
The Owners are Barry and Audrey Sterling and Forrest and Kate Tancer. The Winemaker is Forrest Tancer.

Pinot Noir and Chardonnay are grown at the Iron Horse Vineyards, and Cabernet Sauvignon and Sauvignon Blanc are grown at their other vineyard in the Alexander Valley.

The varietal, vintage-dated, Estate-bottled wines produced are: Chardonnay, Blanc de Pinot Noir, Cabernet Sauvignon and Pinot Noir.

ITALIAN SWISS COLONY
(See Colony)

J

JACARÉ
(See United Vintners)

JADE
(See Turgeon & Lohr)

JADE MOUNTAIN WINERY
1335 Hiatt Road, Cloverdale, CA 95425
Sonoma County
Founded 1975. Owner, Douglas Sebastian Cartwright, M.D.; Vineyard, 26 acres.

JEKEL VINEYARD
40155 Walnut Ave., Greenfield, CA 93927
Monterey County
Storage: Oak and st. steel
Founded 1978. The Owners are Bill and Gus Jekel. The Winemaker is Daniel Lee. The vineyard is located at the winery.

The varietal, vintage-dated wines produced are: Chardonnay, Gamay, Beaujolais, Pinot Blanc, Johannisberg Riesling and Cabernet Sauvignon.

J. F. J. WINERY
(See J. F. J. Bronco Winery)

Johannisberg Riesling
(White Riesling) A varietal grape that produces a fruity-floral, slight-greenish tinge, slightly tart piquant wine, with a touch of sweetness. The ideal wine for clams, crabs and seafood. Its botanic name in California is White Riesling. This is the premier grape of the great vineyards of Germany. The late harvest versions are made from over-ripe grapes, are thick, sweet and long lasting social wines competitive with German Ausleses. Look for the following Johannisberg Riesling: Beringer, Burgess, Callaway, Concannon, Chateau Montelena, Chateau St. Jean, Chapellet, Durney, Firestone, Felton Empire, Freemark Abbey, Geyser Peak, Gundlach-Bundschu, Giumarra, Grgich Hills, Hacienda, Heitz, Jekel, Landmark, Lords & Elwood, Paul Masson Pinnacles, Robert Mondavi, Monterey Vineyards, Joseph Phelps, Raymond, San Martin, Santa Ynez Clos du Bois, Son-

oma, Simi, Souverain, Smith-Madrone, Sanford & Benedict, Sebastiani, Stony Hill, Trefethen, Turgeon-Lohr, Wente.

Look for the following Johannisberg Riesling "Late Harvest": Chateau St. Jean, Chateau Montelena, Concannon, Durney, Firestone, Felton Empire, Freemark Abbey, Grgich Hills, Gundlach-Bundschu, Hoffman Mt. Ranch, Monterey Vineyards, Jekel, Joseph Phelps, Raymond, Smothers, Zaca Mesa.

JOHNSON'S ALEXANDER VALLEY WINES

8333 Hwy 128, Healdsburg, CA 95448

Sonoma County

Storage: Oak and st. steel

The Owners are Jay, Tom and Will Johnson. The Winemaker is Tom Johnson. Purchased in 1952 by James Johnson and sold to his sons in 1971. Vineyard located at southern end of Alexander Valley.

100% Varietal, vintage-dated, Estate-bottled wines produced are Chenin Blanc, Chardonnay, Gewurztraminer, Johannisberg Riesling, Pinot Noir, Cabernet Sauvignon and Zinfandel. Also pear wine. Also produced under J. D. Martin label is Alexander Valley Red.

The Winemaker's favorite wines are Late Harvest Zinfandel and Chenin Blanc.

JORDAN VINEYARD AND WINERY

1474 Alexander Valley Road, Healdsburg, CA 95448

Sonoma County

Founded 1976. The Owner is Thomas N. Jordan, Jr. The Winemaker is Michael Rowan. The vineyard is located at the winery in the Alexander Valley. The new winery and "Chateau" are architecturally exquisite.

The varietal, vintage-dated, Estate-bottled wine produced is Cabernet Sauvignon (8% Merlot). Chardonnay will be the only other wine produced by Jordan. All wines are very carefully made in the French style.

Jug Wines

The dictionary definition of jug is "a vessel in various forms for holding liquids commonly having a handle, often a lip or spout, sometimes with a narrow neck stopped by a cork." My definition is a fair to excellent table wine selling at a moderate price in 1.5, 3 and 4 liter bottles. Homage must be paid to E & J Gallo for their outstanding contribution in making Jug Wines far superior to the general inferior European "vin ordinaire." Today we find not only generic but also varietals and often vintage dated 'Jugs.' No telling what 1990 will bring.

Look for: Jugs White: Barengo French Colombard, Beringer Los Hermanos Chablis, Beaulieu "BV" Chablis, Richard Carey Chenin Blanc, Christian Bros. Chablis, Colony Rhine & French Colombard, Fetzer Premium White, Gallo Chablis Blanc, Inglenook Chablis, Paul Masson Chablis, Lawrence White Table Wine, Parducci Chablis, Petri Chablis Blanc, Robert Mondavi (R. M.) White, Sebastiani Mountain Chablis, Taylor California Cellars, Jug Chablis. Martini and Prati Sauterne, Parducci Vintage Chablis, Royal Host Dry Sauterne, Giumarra Mountain Chablis. Jugs Red: Alamaden Mountain Burgundy, Beaulieu Vineyards Burgundy, Colony Cabernet and Zinfandel, Richard Carey Cabernet Sauvignon, Cribari Cabernet Sauvignon, C. K. Mondavi Zinfandel, Emile's, Fetzer Premium Red, Franciscan Burgundy, Foppiano Burgundy, Gallo Hearty Burgundy, Geyser Peak Napa Gamay and Chianti, Inglenook Navalle Burgundy, Robert Mondavi (R. M.) Red, Sebastiani Mountain Burgundy, Taylor California Cellars, Burgundy, Giumarra Burgundy. Other types: Gibson Fruit Wines, Barengo Sherry, Bargetto's Vin Rosé , Robert Mondavi (R. M.) Rose, San Martin Vin Rosé, Foppiano Vin Rosé.

K

KALIN CELLARS
61 Galli Drive, Novato, CA 94947
Marin County
Owners, J. K. Howard and T. J. Leighton; Winemaker, T. J. Leighton.

KENDALL CELLARS
(See Kalin Cellars)

KATHERYN KENNEDY WINES
13180 Pierce Road, Saratoga, CA 95070
Santa Clara County
The Owner is Katheryn Kennedy; Winemaker is Bill Anderson; Vineyard, 8 acres. The vineyard is located at the winery.

Varietal, vintage-dated wine produced is Cabernet Sauvignon.

ROBERT KEENAN WINERY
3660 Spring Mountain Road, St. Helena, CA 94574
Napa County
Storage: French oak
Owner is Robert Keenan; Winemaker is Joe Cafaro. The vineyard is located at the winery. Vineyard was purchased in 1891. The winery was built in 1904. Robert Keenan purchased the property in 1974.

The wines produced are vintage-dated varietals. Napa Valley Cabernet Sauvignon, Napa Valley Pinot Noir, Napa Valley Chardonnay and Sonoma County Chardonnay.

KENWOOD VINEYARDS
9592 Sonoma Hwy., Kenwood, CA 95452
Sonoma County
Storage: American and French oak, st. steel
Founded 1906. The owner is a corporation of which John Sheela is President and Martin Lee is Vice President. Winemakers are Robert Kozlowski and Mike Lee. Vineyard is located at winery. Grapes are also purchased from selected vineyards.

Varietal, vintage-dated wines produced are Pinot Noir, Zinfandel, Petite Sirah, Cabernet Sauvignon, Chardonnay, Pinot Noir Blanc, Dry Chenin Blanc, Johannisberg Riesling, Cabernet Sauvignon Blanc, and Pinot Noir Rosé. Also generic Burgundy and Chablis.

Winemaker's favorite wine is "Jack London" Cabernet Sauvignon.

KENWORTHY VINEYARDS
Route 2, Box 2, Plymouth, CA 95669
Amador County
Storage: Oak and st. steel
Owner and Winemaker is John Kenworthy; Vineyards are in Amador County; Shenandoah.
Varietal wines produced are Zinfandel, Cabernet Sauvignon and Chardonnay.

KERN COUNTY
(Southern San Joaquin Valley) Wines to look for: Giumarra Vineyards, La Mont Winery, A. Perelli-Minetti & Sons.

KIRIGIN CELLARS
11550 Watsonville Road, Gilroy, CA 95020
Santa Clara County
Storage: Oak, redwood and st. steel
Founded 1916. The Owners are Nikola Kirigin Chargin, Sr. and Jr. The Winemaker is Nikola Sr, a fourth generation winemaker from Yugoslavia where he started in his family vineyard. The vineyard is located at the winery in the Uvas Valley.

The varietal, vintage-dated wines produced are French Colombard, White Riesling, Pinot Chardonnay, Sauvignon Vert, Malvasia Bianca, Gewurztraminer, Chenin Blanc, Pinot Noir, Zinfandel and Cabernet Sauvignon.

Also produced are Opal Rosé, Champagne, Chablis, Rhine, Rosé, Burgundy, Sherry and Port.

KIRKHAM FAMILY WINERY
3473 Silverado Trail, St. Helena, CA 94574
Napa County

KIRKWOOD
(See Barengo Vineyards)

KISTLER VINEYARDS
2995 Nelligan Rd., Glen Ellen, CA 95442
Sonoma County
Storage: French oak and st. steel
Owner and Winemaker is Stephen Kistler; Vineyard in Napa Valley and Sonoma County.
Varietal wines produced are Chardonnay, Cabernet Sauvignon and Pinot Noir.

Kleinberger Riesling
(White Table Wine) A varietal grape which produces a light and delicate wine.

KONOCTI CELLARS
4350 Thomas Drive, Kelseyville, CA 95451
Lake County
Storage: Oak and st. steel
Owners, a cooperative of Lake County vintners; Winemaker, Wm. T. Pease; Vineyards are located in Lake County   *(continued)*

Varietal wines produced are Cabernet Sauvignon, Johannisberg Riesling, Zinfandel, Cabernet Sauvignon Blanc, Cabernet Rose, Soft Zinfandel and Cabernet Franc.

F. KORBEL AND BROS.

13250 River Road, Guerneville, CA 95446
Sonoma County
Storage: Oak and st. steel
The Owner is Adolph L. Heck. The Winemaker is Jim Huntsinger. The vineyards are located in western Sonoma County. The first section of the present winery was built in 1881 by the Korbel Bros. In 1954, Adolph Heck bought the winery. He had been a Champagne maker and was President of Italian Swiss Colony. Distributed nationally by Jack Daniels. The Champagnes produced are Natural, Blanc de Noirs, Brut, Extra Dry, Sec, Rouge and Rosé. Also known for their Brandy. Recommend: Blanc de Noirs Champagne.

HANNS KORNELL CHAMPAGNE CELLARS

1091 Larkmead Lane, St. Helena, CA 94574
Napa County
Owner and Winemaker is Hanns Kornell. A third generation Champagne Master, Hanns Kornell came from Germany in 1940 and started his cellars in 1952. Grapes are purchased on a selected vineyard basis.

The Champagnes produced are bottle fermented and aged in the original bottle. They are Extra-dry, Brut, Demi-Sec, Pink Rosé, Rouge Muscat Alexandria and the internationally award winning Sehr Trocken.

CHARLES KRUG WINERY

P.O. Box 191, Hwy. #29, St. Helena, CA 94574
Napa County
The Owners are Peter Mondavi and Mrs. Mary Westbrook (sister). Vineyards are located in the Napa Valley. The oldest operating winery in the valley, established by Charles Krug in 1861.

The wines produced under the Charles Krug label are 95% varietal. They are Cabernet Sauvignon (vintage), Zinfandel, Gamay Beaujolais, Pinot Noir, Grey Riesling, Johannisberg Riesling, Blanc Fume, Chenin Blanc, Pinot Chardonnay, Gewurztraminer and Muscat Canelli. Also produced are Burgundy, Claret, Vin Rose and Chablis.

The wines produced under the C. K. Mondavi label (jug wines) are Chablis, Rhine, Dry Sauterne, Vin Rosé, Burgundy, Barverone, Fortissimo, Bravissimo, Claret, Chianti, Light Burgundy and Zinfandel.

The Winemaker's favorite are the Charles Krug Chenin Blanc and Cabernet Sauvignon (Vintage Select).

THOMAS KRUSE WINERY

4390 Hecker Pass Road, Gilroy, CA 95020
Santa Clara County
Storage: Oak, redwood and st. steel
Owner and Winemaker is Thomas Kruse.

Varietal wines produced are Cabernet Sauvignon, Chardonnay and Zinfandel and even a Thompson Seedless called "Chutzpah." Also produced is a methode champenoise Champagne.

L

Label Reading

Vintage Date: To carry a vintage date, a wine must be made from 95% of the grapes harvested during that year.

Appellation of Origin: At least 75% of the grapes used in the wine were grown in the named region (either state or county). If the label indicates a specific "viticultural area" (i.e. vineyard or ranch name) the wine must contain 95% of the grapes from that area.

Wine Type: The name of the grape that inspired the wine except in the case of generic wines. The wine must have been made from at least 51% of that particular grape. (In 1983, the requirement rises to 75%). Any other wine other than a varietal name (Burgundy, Rhine, etc.) has no regulations as to what grape is used.

LAKE COUNTY

(North of Napa County) Wines to look for: Konocti Cellars, Lower Lake.

LA CREMA VINERA

1250 Holm Rd., Petaluma, CA 94952

Sonoma County

Storage: French oak and st. steel

Owners are Rod Berglund, Bob Goyette, John Bessey and Rick Burmester. Grapes purchased on a select vineyard basis. Winemaker, Rod Berglund.

Varietal, vintage dated wines produced are Pinot Noir-Winery Lake, Ventana, Cabernet Sauvignon-Steiner Vineyards (Sonoma), Chardonnay-Winery Lake (Carnepos), Ventana (Monterey).

LA CROIX

(See Bisceglia Bros.)

LAKE SPRING WINERY

Hoffman Lane, Yountville, CA 94599

(707) 963-2483

Napa County

RONALD LAMB VINEYARDS AND WINERY

17785 Casa Lane, Morgan Hill, CA 95037

Santa Clara County

Storage: Oak barrels

Owners are Ronald and Aldrene Lamb. The Winemaker is Ronald Lamb. The vineyard is located in Santa Clara County. Grapes are also purchased on a select vineyard basis.

Varietal, vintage-dated wines produced are Ventana Vineyards Dry Johannisberg Riesling, Monterey County, Napa Gamay (Ventana Vineyards), Sonoma Gamay Beaujolais, San Luis Obispo County Zinfandel, Santa Clara Zinfandel, Chardonnay and Chenin Blanc.

Winemaker's favorite wine is Amador County Zinfandel.

LAMBERT BRIDGE

4085 West Dry Creek Road, Healdsburg, CA 95448
Sonoma County
Storage: Oak and st. steel
Founded 1979. The Owner is Gerard B. Lambert. The Winemaker is Dominic Martin. Vineyard, 78 acres. The vineyards are located in the Central Dry Creek Valley.

Varietal, vintage-dated, Estate-bottled wines produced are Chardonnay and Cabernet Sauvignon.

M. LAMONT WINERY

Bear Mountain Winery Road, DiGiorgio, CA
Kern County
Storage: Oak, redwood & st. steel
Founded 1966. The winery is owned by John La Batt, Ltd. Breweries of Canada. Purchases grapes on a selected region basis. Winemaker: Sam Balakian.

Varietal wines produced are Chenin Blanc, French Colombard, Rosé of Barbera, Ruby Cabernet, Zinfandel, Gewurztraminer, Chardonnay and Green Hungarian.

Generic wines produced are Chablis, Rhine, Burgundy and Vin Rosé. Also produced is "Black Monua" cream sherry.

LA MONTANA

(See Martin Ray Vineyard)

LA MOUTONNE NOIRE

(See Richard Carey Winery)

LANDMARK VINEYARDS

9150 Los Amigos Road, Windsor, CA 95492
Sonoma County
Storage: Limousin and st. steel
Founded 1974. The Owner is the William R. Mabry family. The Winemaker is William R. Mabry III. Vineyards are located in Alexander Valley, Sonoma and Windsor.

The 100% varietal, vintage-dated wines produced are Chardonnay, Pinot Noir, Cabernet Sauvignon and Chenin Blanc.

LANDIS VINEYARD

2068 E. Clayton Ave., Fresno, CA 93725
Fresno County
18 acres producing Table Wines.

MAMO LANZA

(See Wooden Valley Winery)

LA PURISMA WINERY

725 Sunnyvale-Saratoga Rd., Sunnyvale, CA 94087
Santa Clara County
Owner and Winemaker, Doug Watson; Vineyards, 40 acres.

LAS TABLAS WINERY

P. O. Box 697, Winery Road, Templeton, CA 93465
San Luis Obispo County
The Owners are John and Della Mertens. John is the Winemaker. The Mertens are the third family to own Las Tablas since it was started in 1856. The vineyard is located at the winery.

Wines produced are Zinfandel, Rosé, White table wine and Sweet Muscat.

LA QUESTA
(See Woodside Vineyards)

DOMAINE LAURIER
(See Shilo Vineyards)

LAWRENCE WINERY
P.O. Box 698, San Luis Obispo, CA 93406
San Luis Obispo County
Storage: Oak, redwood and st. steel
Founded 1978. Owners are James S. Lawrence, Herman L. Dreyers and Donald S. Burns. The Winemaker is James S. Lawrence. The vineyards are in San Luis Obispo and Santa Barbara Counties.

100% varietal, Estate-bottled, vintage-dated wines produced are Gamay Beaujolais, Gewurztraminer, Gewurztraminer Rosé, Johannisberg Riesling, Pinot Noir, Sauvignon Blanc, White Riesling, Zinfandel, Cabernet Sauvignon and Chardonnay.

Estate-bottled 100% varietals produced are Chenin Blanc and Fume Blanc.

Varietals, Estate-bottled are French Colombard, Grenache Rosé, and Semillon. Also produced are Red Table Wine (Napa Gamay, Pinot Noir, Grenache, Gamay Beajolais and Zinfandel), White Table Wine (French Colombard, Sauvignon Blanc and Chardonnay), Rosé Table Wine (Napa Gamay and Grenache).

The Winemaker's favorite wines are Johannisberg Riesling, Gewurztraminer, Chenin Blanc and Sauvignon Blanc.

LAZY CREEK VINEYARD
4610 Hwy. 128, Philo, CA 95466
Mendocino County
Manager, Johann J. Kobler; Vineyards, 20 acres.

LE BLANC
(See California Growers Winery)

L. LE BLANC VINEYARDS
(See California Growers Winery)

LE DOMAINE
Bottle fermented Champagne. (See Almaden Vineyards)

Lees
Yeast sediment deposited by wine in the cooperage after fermentation.

LEEWARD WINERY
2511 Victoria Ave, Channel Isalnds Harbor, CA 93030
Ventura County
Storage: American and French oak, st. steel
Owners and Winemakers are Chuck Brigham and Chuck Gardner.

Grapes are purchased on a select vineyard basis. Varietal, vintage dated wines produced are Zinfandel (Amador County), Chardonnay (San Luis Obispo), Cabernet Sauvignon (San Luis Obispo).

LE FLEURON-
(See Joseph Phelps Vineyards)

CHARLES LE FRANC
(See Almaden Vineyards)

LEJON
(Champagne and Vermouth brand) (See United Vintners)

LIBERTY
(See Rubidoux Winery)

LIBERTY SCHOOL
(See Caymus Vineyards)

LIBERTY WINERY
6055 E. Acampo Road, Acampo, CA 95220
San Joaquin County
Founded 1946. Owner, Herbert Buck; Winemaker, Chester G. Kreis. Primarily Bulk and Wholesale.

LIVE OAKS WINERY
3875 Hecker Pass Hwy., Gilroy, CA 95020
Santa Clara County
Storage: Oak, redwood, st. steel
Established 1974. Owner is Peter Scagliotti. Winemaker is Mitsuo Takemoto. The vineyards are located at the winery in the Santa Clara Valley. The vineyard was planted by Peter's father Eduardo in 1912.

Wines produced are "Premium Quality" Burgundy (aged 65 months), Sauterne, Haut Sauterne, Grenache Rosé and Chenin Blanc (medium).

LIVERMORE VALLEY CELLARS
1508 Wetmore Road, Livermore, CA 94550
Alameda County
Storage: Oak
Owner and Winemaker, Chris Lagiss; Vineyards are in Livermore Valley
Varietal wines produced are Pinot Blanc, Riesling, French Colombard and Golden Chasselas.

J. LOHR
(See Turgeon-Lohr Winery)

LONG VINEYARDS
P. O. Box 50, St. Helena, CA 94574
Napa County
Storage: Oak and st. steel
Owners are Robert and Zelma Long. The Winemaker is Robert Long. The vineyard is located at the winery.

Varietal, vintage-dated, Estate-Bottled wines produced are Johannisberg Riesling and Chardonnay. Wines sold from waiting list only.

LLORDS & ELWOOD WINERY
P.O. Box 3397, Fremont, CA 94538
Alameda County
Storage: Oak and outdoors Sherry solera
Founded 1955. Owner is the Elwood Family. The Winemaker is Richard H. Elwood. Grapes are purchased on a select vineyard basis. The first in California to develop a commercially successful Spanish type Solera for ageing sherries. Also pioneered rosé made from Cabernet Sauvignon grapes and late-harvest style Johannisberg Riesling.

The varietal, vintage-dated wines produced are the Rare Chardonnay, Castel Magic Johannisberg Riesling, Rosé of Cabernet, Velvet Hills Pinot Noir and Cabernet

Sauvignon. Also produced are Great Day D-r-ry Sherry, Dry Wit Sherry, the Judge's Secret Cream Sherry and Ancient Proverb Port.

LOS ALAMOS
(See Hale Cellars)

LOS ANGELES COUNTY
(Southern California) Ahern Winery, The Martin Winery, San Antonio Winery

LOS ANGELES, ORANGE

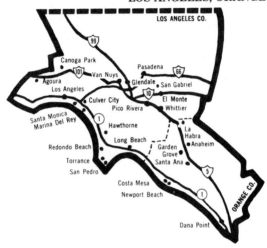

Los Altos
(See B & R Vineyards)

LOS COCHES CELLARS
(See Ventana Vineyards Winery)

LOS HERMANOS
(See Beringer Vineyards)

LOST HILLS VINEYARDS
3050 Brundage Lane, Bakersfield, CA 93304
Kern County
The Owner is Herbert R. Benham, Jr. President of Berrenda Mesa Farming. The Winemaker is Curt R. Meyer. Lost Hills Vineyards is only a 1,500 acre part in a complex 26,000 acre farming operation. Grapes are also purchased on a select vineyard basis.

Varietal, vintage-dated wines produced are Napa Valley Cabernet Sauvignon, Napa Valley Johannisberg Riesling and Napa Valley Pinot Chardonnay.

Varietals produced are Chenin Blanc, Cabernet Sauvignon and Gamay Rosé. Also produced are White, Red and Rosé.

Louis 5th
(See California Wine Co.)

LOWER LAKE WINERY

P.O. Box 950, Hwy, 29, Lower Lake, CA 95457
Lake County
Storage: French oak and st. steel
The Owners are Harry, Marjorie, Daniel and Elizabeth
Stuermer and Thomas and Harriet Scavone. The Wine-
maker is Daniel H. Stuermer, Ph.D. Grapes are pur-
chased from select Lake County Vineyards.

100% varietal, vintage-dated wines produced are Cabernet Sauvignon and Sauvignon Blanc.

LUCAS HOME WINE

18196 N. Davis, Lodi, CA 95240
San Joaquin County
Founded 1978. Owners, David and Tamara Lucas; Winemaker, David Lucas; Vineyards, 30 acres. Varietal wine
produced is Zinfandel.

LYTTON SPRINGS WINERY

650 Lytton Springs Road, Healdsburg, CA 95448
Sonoma County
The Owners are Walt Walters and Dee Sindt. Grapes are
purchased on a select vineyard basis. Valley Vista vineyard is located at the winery.

Varietal, vintage-dated wines produced are "Valley
Vista" Zinfandel, "Russian River" Cabernet Sauvignon
and Gewurztraminer. Recommend: Zinfandel.

M

Madeira

A rich fortified wine of the Sherry class, originally from
the island of Madeira. It is made from white grapes and
has additional sugar added for sweetening.

MADERA COUNTY

(Mid San Joaquin Valley) Wines to look for: Bisceglia
Bros., Coarsegold, Papagni, Quady, Ficklin.

MADRIA-MADRIA

(See E & J Gallo)

Malbec

One of the three great Bordeaux grapes. Long lasting,
tannic. Usually blended with Cabernet Sauvignon. Look
for: Veedercrest Vineyards.

Malvasia Bianca

(White Table and Dessert Wine) A varietal grape that
because of its sweetness is used for dessert wines or
sweet table wine. Also used for Asti Spumante style
sparkling wines. Originally imported from the Asti region of Italy. Look for: San Martin, Novitiate.

DONNAMARIA VINEYARD

10286 Chalf Hill Rd., Healdsburg, CA 95448
Sonoma County

MARIN COUNTY

(North Central Coast) Wines to look for: Far Niente
Winery, Pacheco Ranch Winery, Woodbury Winery.

MARKHAM WINERY

2812 North St. St. Helena Hwy., St. Helena, CA 94574
Napa County
Storage: Limousin oak and st. steel
Founded 1978. Owners are H. Bruce and Kate Markham.
The Winemaker is Bryan Del Bondio. Vineyards are in
four acres of Napa Valley.

Wines produced are 100% varietal, estate-bottled.
They are Chenin Blanc, Johannisberg Riesling, Muscat
de Frontignan, Gamay Beaujolais, Merlot and Gamay
Beaujolais Blanc.

MARTIN WINERY

11800 West Jefferson Blvd, Culver City, CA 90230
Owners and Winemakers are Chuck Martin and Jim
Humphries. Own no vineyards. Produce wines under la-
bel names: Martin, Chateau Martin and St. Martin. Also
champagne and Brandy. No connectionwith San Martin
Winery.

LOUIS M. MARTINI

P. O. Box 112, St. Helena, CA 94574
Napa County
Storage: American oak, redwood and st. steel
Founded 1923. The winery is owned by the Martini fam-
ily. The Winemakers are Louis P. and Michael R. Mar-
tini, son and grandson of the founder. There are two
vineyards in Napa County, in the Carneros Region and
Chilies Valley. Two vineyards in Sonoma County are on
Mayacamas Mountains and near Healdsburg. The var-
ietal wines produced are Cabernet Sauvignon, Pinot
Noir, Merlot, Barbera, Zinfandel, Gamay Beaujolias,
Pinot Chardonnay, Johannisberg Riesling, Gewurztraminer, Folle Blanche, Dry Chenin Blanc.

The generics produced are Burgundy, Claret, Chianti,
Chablis, Mountain Red, Mountain White, Mountain Vin
Rose, Pale Dry and Cream Sherry. Occasionally limited
amounts of Private Reserve and Special Selection wines
are produced.

Winemaker's favorites are the special Selection Cabernet Sauvignon and Pinot Chardonnay "Special Lot"
and Merlot.

MARTINI & PRATI WINES

2191 Laguana Rd., Santa Rosa, CA 95401
Sonoma County
Storage: Oak, redwood and cement
Owners are Elmo Martini and Edward Prati. Originally
founded in the early 1900's when their Fountain Grove
label became famous. The winery is operated once again
by members of the original family. Winemaker: Frank
J. Vannucci.

Varietal wines produced are Zinfandel, Gamay Beau-
jolais, Pinot Noir, Petite Sirah, Merlot, Chenin Blanc,
Grey Riesling and French Colombard. Also produced are
Sparkling Burgundy and Champagne.

PAUL MASSON VINEYARDS

13150 Saratoga Avenue, Saratoga, CA 95070
Santa Clara and Monterey County   (continued)

Storage: Oak, redwood and st. steel

Paul Masson is a subsidiary of the House of Seagram. The Winemaker is Joseph Stillman. The history of Paul Masson begins in 1852, when Etienne Thee, a vigneron from Bordeaux, came to California and planted a vineyard south of San Jose, thus pioneering winegrowing in the Santa Clara Valley. He was succeeded by his son-in-law, Paul Masson, a native of Beaune in the Burgundy district of France. Masson retired in 1936 and the House of Seagram acquired the vineyards in 1943. Paul Masson vineyard holdings are close to 5,000 acres.

Varietal, vintage-dated, Estate-bottled "Pinnacles" wines are Gewurztraminer, Johannisberg Riesling, Chardonnay, Fumé, Blanc and Johannisberg Riesling Champagne.

Varietal wines produced are Johannisberg Riesling, Pinot Blanc, Zinfandel, Chenin Blanc, Pinot Chardonnay, Cabernet Sauvignon, Pinot Noir, Gamay Beaujolais, Petite Sirah, Riesling, French Colombard and Gamay Rosé. Also produced are Burgundy, Chablis, Rosé, Rhine, Dry Sauterne, Vin Rosé Sec, Rhine Castle Emerald Dry, Rubion Claret Baroque Burgundy, Sangria, Port, Sherry, Madeira, Very Cold Duck, Crackling Rosé and Crackling Chablis (both Sparkling Wines). Sparkling wines produced are Champagne Brut, Pink and Extra Dry Pink and Sparkling Burgundy.

The Winemaker's favorite wines are the varietal, Estate-bottled "Pinnacles."

MASTANTUONO WINERY

101-¾ Willow Creek Road, Paso Robles, CA 93446
San Luis Obispo County
Storage: American oak and st. steel
Founded 1977. The Owner and Winemaker is Pasquale A. Mastan. Vineyard is in hills west of Templeton. Only wine produced is varietal, vintage-dated, Estate-bottled Zinfandel.

MATANZAS CREEK WINERY

6097 Bennett Valley Road, Santa Rosa, CA 95404
SonomaCounty
Storage: French oak and st. steel
Founded 1978. The Owner is Sandra S. Steiner. The Winemaker is Merry Edwards. Vineyards are on Sonoma Mountain at about 1000 feet and the base of Bennett Peak in Bennett Valley. Some grapes are also purchased on a select vineyard basis primarily in Sonoma County.

Varietal, vintage-dated wines produced are Chardonnay, Pinot Noir, Merlot and Cabernet Sauvignon. Also produced on a limited basis are Pinot Blanc, Gewurztraminer, Sauvignon Blanc and Semillion.

MATHEWS NAPA VALLEY WINERY

1711 Main St., Napa, CA 94588
Founded 1866. Owners, Kenneth and Barbara Nelson. Winemaker is Kenneth Nelson. Varietal wines produced are Cabernet Sauvignon, Chardonnay, Zinfandel, Chenin Blanc. Also produced are Tokay, Tawny Port and Sherries.

MAYACAMAS VINEYARDS
1155 Lokoya Road, Napa, CA 94558
Napa County
Storage: oak
Founded 1889. Owners are Robert B. and Elinor D. Travers. Robert is the Winemaker. The vineyards are located at the winery. The original winery was built in 1889. Mayacamas, where the winery is, is the name of the mountain range that separates the Napa and Sonoma Valleys.

The estate-bottled, vintage-dated varietal wines produced are Chardonnay and Cabernet Sauvignon. Also produced are varietal Late-Harvest Zinfandel, Pinot Noir and Sauvignon Blanc.

GIUSEPPE MAZZONI
Rt. A, Box 47, Cloverdale, CA 95425
Sonoma County
Storage: Redwood
Founded 1912. Owners, Fred and James Mazzoni; Vineyards, 150 acres in Sonoma County. Wines produced are Dry Burgundy and Sauterne.

MCDOWELL VALLEY VINEYARDS
3811 Hwy 175, Hopland, CA 95449
Mendocino County
Storage: Oak barrels
The Owners are Rich and Karen Keehn. The Winemaker is George Bursick. The original ranch was built by Paxton McDowell in the mid-1800s. The winery is solar integrated. The vineyard is located at the winery.

100% varietal, vintage-dated, Estate-bottled wines produced are Grenache, dry Chenin Blanc, Chardonnay, Sauvignon Blanc, French Colombard, Cabernet Sauvignon, Petite Sirah, Zinfandel, Carignane.

Mellow
Soft in taste, term used to describe "Vino Rosso" red dinner wines. Also sometimes used to designate well-matured Sherries, wines containing some sweetness.

MENDOCINO COUNTY
Appellations: (Northern Coast) Anderson Valley and Redwood Valley. Wines to look for: Cresta Blanca, Dach, Edmeades, Fetzer, Husch, McDowell Valley, Milano Winery, Navarro, Parducci, Tyland Vineyards, Weibel.

Merlot
(A Red Table Wine) A varietal grape that produces a distinctive aromatic, spicy, medium red in color wine with some of the green olive and herbaceous odor of Cabernet Sauvignon. Originally from the Bordeaux region of France where it is a major factor in the wines of Pommerd and St. Emilion. Look for: Louis Martini, Chateau St. Jean, Richard Carey, Stags Leap, Sterling, Z-D.

Metallic
A defect in wine. A hint of bitterness, a hard finish.

Microclimates and Quality
This is no end all of facts. For the most part, the grapes have the best love affairs in these regions. Like all love affairs, there are exceptions.   *(continued)*

MENDOCINO, SONOMA

Coldest Climates: Santa Cruz, Santa Maria, Sonoma, Upper Monterey; Pinot Noir, Pinot Blanc, Johannisberg Riesling, Gewurztraminer, Grey Riesling.

Medium Cool: Monterey, Napa Carneros, Santa Barbara, Sonoma: Pinot Blanc, Chardonnay, Sylvaner, Grenache, Grey Riesling, Johannisberg Riesling, Petite Sirah, Zinfandel (sometimes).

Medium Warm: Lower Monterey, San Luis Obispo, Upper Napa Valley; Semillon, Sauvignon Blanc, Chenin Blanc, Zinfandel, Cabernet Sauvignon, Petite Sirah, Grenache, Napa Gamay, French Colombard, Chandonay (sometimes).

Hot Climates: (Central Valley) Bakersfield, Fresno, Lodi, Modesto; French Colombard, Ruby Cabernet, Barbera, Carrignane, Palomino, Tinta Madera, Grenache.

MILANO WINERY

14594 South Hwy 101, Hopland, CA 95449
Mendocino County
Storage: Oak, redwood and st. steel
The Owners and Winemakers are James Milone and Gregory Graziano. The families vineyards go back to early 1900s. Vineyard is located in Redwood Valley, Grapes are also purchased from select vineyard in Anderson Valley.

Varietal, vintage-dated wines produced are Chardonnay, Sauvignon Blanc, Chenin Blanc, Cabernet Sauvignon, Zinfandel, Gamay Beaujolais and Petite Sirah.

The Winemaker's favorite wines are Chardonnay, Cabernet Sauvignon and Zinfandel.

MILL CREEK VINEYARDS

1401 Westside Road, Healdsburg, CA 95448 *(continued)*

Sonoma County
Storage: American and French oak, st. steel
The Owners are Charles, William and James Kreck. The Winemaker is James Kreck. Vineyard is located at winery in Dry Creek Valley.

Varietal, vintage-dated, Estate-bottled wines produced are Cabernet Sauvignon, Cabernet Blush, (Rosé) (100% Cabernet Sauvignon), Chardonnay (100%), Pinot Noir (100%), Merlot and Gamay Beaujolais (100%) and Burgundy Balnc, Blanc de Noir, (100% Pinot Noir).

The Winemaker's favorite wines are the Cabernet Sauvignon, Chardonnay and Cabernet Blush.

F. J. MILLER
8329 St. Helena Hwy., Napa, CA 94558
Napa County
The Owner and Winemaker is F. Justin Miller. The winery was established in 1960 in order to demonstrate his "Miller Way" method of carbonating a still wine, in the bottle, without recourse to fermentation of sugar added to the wine. Wines produced are effervescent.

MIRASSOU VINEYARDS
3000 Aborn Road, San Jose, CA 95121
Santa Clara and Monterey Counties
Storage: Oak, redwood and st. steel
Founded 1854. The Owners are the Mirassou family. The Winemaker is Don Alexander. Vineyards are located in selected districts.

Varietal, vintage-dated wines produced are Chardonnay, Chenin Blanc, Gewurztraminer, Johannisberg Riesling, Monterey Riesling, Cabernet Sauvignon, Gamay Beaujolais, Petite Sirah, Pinot Noir, Zinfandel and Monterey Zinfandel. Also produced are Dry Chablis, Fleuri Blanc, White Burgundy, Petite Rosé, and Burgundy and Champagne. Recommend: Monterey Riesling, Monterey Chardonnay and Monterey Zinfandel.

C. K. MONDAVI
(See Charles Krug Winery)

ROBERT MONDAVI WINERY
7801 St. Helena Hwy, Oakville, CA 94562
Napa County
Storage: Oak and st. steel
Founded 1966. Owner is the Mondavi Family. Robert is Chm. of the Board and Michael is President. The Winemakers are Robert and Tim Mondavi. Tim is in charge of production. The vineyards are located at the winery and in selected districts.

Varietal, vintage-dated wines produced are Fumé Blanc, Chardonnay, Johannisberg Riesling, Chenin Blanc, Gamay Rosé, Napa Gamay, Pinot Noir, Cabernet Sauvignon, Zinfandel and Muscato D'Oro.

Also produced is R. M. vintage Red, White and Rosé.

MONTCLAIR WINERY
180 Maxwelton Road, Piedmont, CA 94618
Alameda County
Storage: oak
Founded 1975

Owners are R. K. Dove, L. A. Dorie and J. H. Burkhard. The Winemaker is R. K. Dove. Also wines under the "Big Foot" label.

Varietal type wines produced are Zinfandel, Cabernet Sauvignon and French Colombard.

MONT D'EDE L'ESCANTE

(See Endgate Vineyards)

MONTE CARLO VINEYARDS

1537 Powell St., San Francisco, CA 94133

Founded 1933. Owner, Norman Peri. Cellars and bottles various Italian style wines from Sonoma County.

MONTEREY COUNTY

(Central Coast) Appellations: Carmel Valley, Soledad and Arroyo Seco. Wines to look for: Almaden, Carmel Bay, Chalone, Durney, Jekel, Paul Masson Pinnacles, Mirassou, Monterey Peninsula, Rapuzzini, San Martin, The Monterey Vineyard, Turgeon & Lohr, Ventana, Wente Bros., Zampattis.

MONTEREY PENINSULA WINERY

2999 Monterey Salinas Hwy., Monterey, CA 93940
Monterey County
Storage: American and French oak
Founded 1974. The owners are Roy Thomas and Deryck Nuckton. The Winemaker is Roy Thomas. Founded in 1974 the winery has won over 80 awards at competitive wine tastings. Grapes are purchased on a select vineyard basis from Monterey, San Luis Obispo and Amador Countires.   *(continued)*

MONTEREY, SAN BENITO, SANTA CLARA, SANTA CRUZ

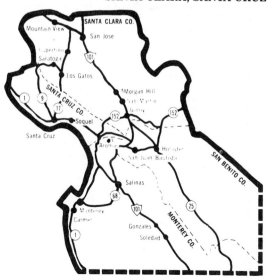

100% varietal, vintage-dated wines produced are Zinfandel, Barbera, Pinot St. George, Chardonnay, Merlot, Pinot Noir, Cabernet Sauvignon, Petite Sirah, Pinot Blanc, Sauvignon Blanc, Botrytised Chenin Blanc, Malvasia Blanca and Muscat Canelli.

Wines produced under the Monterey Cellars label are Dry Chablis, Emerald Riesling, Chablis, California Rosé and Ruby Cabernet. Produced under the Big Sur label are Big Sur white and Red.

The Winemaker's favorite wines are Chardonnay, Cabernet Sauvignon and Zinfandel.

THE MONTEREY VINEYARD
P.O. Box 780, Gonzales, CA 93926
Monterey County
Storage: Oak, redwood, st. steel
Founded 1973. The Owner is The Wine Spectrum (Coca Cola Co. of Atlanta, Ga.). The Winemaker is Richard G. Peterson, Ph.D. Founded by a group of grape growers in 1973, purchased by R. G. Peterson and D.A. Lucas in 1976 and sold to Coca Cola in 1977. Monterey vineyards produces Taylor California Cellars for the Taylor Wine Co. (Also owned by The Wine Spectrum). Only production and quality control are done by Monterey Vineyards. Not the marketing. Only winery to produce generic wines from 100% Coastal County grapes. Peterson is also responsible for producing several wines that were never produced in California before, "January Harvest," "December Harvest," and Botrytis Wines.

Vineyard is in Gonzales, Upper Monterey County. Varietal, vintage-dated wines produced are Chardonnay, Fumé Blanc, Chenin Blanc, Grüner Sylvaner, Gewurztraminer, Johannisberg Riesling, Rosé of Pinot Noir, Rosé of Cabernet Sauvignon, Zinfandel, Pinot Noir and Botrytis Sauvignon Blanc.

Winemaker's favorite wine is Gewurztraminer, Johannisberg Riesling and Chardonnay.

MONTEVINA
Shenandoah School Road, Plymouth, CA 95669
Amador County
Storage: American and French oak, st. steel
Founded 1973. Owners are Gary Gott and W. H. Field. The Winemaker is Gary Gott. Vineyard originally established in 1890's. Located in Shenandoah Valley.
Estate-bottled 100% varietal wines produced are Zinfandel, Buevo (Beaujolais style) and Zinfandel. Also produced are Sauvignon Blanc, White-Zinfandel, White-Cabernet, Barbera, Ruby Cabernet, Cabernet Sauvignon and Zinfandel.

Winemaker's favorite wines are Zinfandel and Sauvignon Blanc.

MONT LA SALLE
(See Christian Brothers)

MONT ST. JOHN CELLARS
5400 Old Sonoma Rd, Napa, CA 94558

J. W. MORRIS PORT WORKS
1215 Park Avenue, Emeryville, CA 94608   *(continued)*

Alameda County
Storage: American oak
Founded 1975
The Owners are James W. Morris, James L. Olsen, Terrill M. Olsen. The Winemaker is James L. Olsen. A new but already medal winning winery.

The wines produced are Founders Port, Early-Bottled Vintage Port, Late-Bottled Vintage Port, Sierra and Sabrosa Angelica.

Varietal, vintage-dated wines produced are Monterey County, Chenin Blanc, Sonoma County Sauvignon Blanc, Sonoma County Cabernet Sauvignon, Sonoma County Zinfandel and Sonoma County Pinot Noir.

The Winemaker's favorite wines are Vintage Port, Sauvignon Blanc and Angelica.

MOUNT EDEN VINEYARDS

22000 Mt. Eden Road, Saratoga, CA 95070
Santa Clara County
Storage: Oak
Founded 1972
Owner is the M.E. V. Corporation. The Winemaker is Richard White. Originally, the Martin Ray Estate Vineyard was in Santa Cruz Mountains at approximately 2000 ft. elevation.

Estate-bottled, varietal wines produced under the Mount Eden Vineyard label are Cabernet Sauvignon, Pinot Noir and Chardonnay. A varietal produced under the MEV lable from Monterey grapes is a Chardonnay.

Winemaker's favorite wines are the Pinot Noir and the Chardonnay. Also the vintage-dated Cabernet Sauvignon.

MOUNT PALOMAR WINERS

33820 Rancho California Road, Temecula, CA 92390
Riverside County
Storage: Oak and st. steel
Founded 1975. Owner is John H. Poole. Winemaker is Joseph E. Cherpin. The vineyard is at the winery in the high country close to Palomar Mountain. Wines produced under the Mount Palomar label are Sauvignon Blanc, White Riesling, Chenin Blanc, Cabernet Rosé, Zinfandel, Rose de Petite Sirah, Cabernet Sauvignon, Petite Sirah and Shiraz. Mount Palomar generics are Vin Blanc (Sauvignon Blanc with Chenin Blanc), Vin Rose (Zinfandel with Chenin Blanc) and Rhine Wine (White Riesling with Chenin Blanc). Mount Palomar dessert wines are Cocktail Sherry (dry), Golden Sherry (medium), Cream Sherry (sweet) and Sweet Cabernet (100% Cabernet Sauvignon). Rancho Temecula-labeled Jug Wines are Chablis, Burgundy, Vin Rose and Sangria.

MOUNT VEEDER WINERY

1999 Mt. Veeder Road, Napa, CA 94558
Napa County
Owners are Michael and Arlene Bernstein. The Winemaker is Michael Bernstein. The vineyards are located on the slopes of Mount Veeder in the Napa Valley.
80% of the wines produced are varietal, vintage-dated,

Estate-bottled Cabernet Sauvignon. The balance is Zinfandel and Chenin Blanc.

MOUNTAIN HOUSE WINERY
3899 Hwy 128, Cloverdale, CA 95425
Mendocino County

The owners are Ronn Lipp and partners. The Mountain House ranch dates back to the 1850s. Vineyard is located at winery. Also, grapes will be purchased on a selected vineyard basis.

Varietal, vintage-dated wines produced are Pinot Blanc, Late Harvest Zinfandel and Chardonnay.

Moscato Canelli
(White Table Wine) A varietal grape, the Moscato produces a rich, fruity wine with a delicate muscat character. Sweet enough to be a dessert wine also. Will age very well. Look for: Louis Martini, Charles Krug, Sutter Home, Estrella Riverra. Also very similar: Muscat Blanc by Inglenook and Concannon.

Mother Lode
(See California Cellar Masters)

Mountain Gold
(See La Mont Winery)

Mountain Peak
(See La Mont Winery)

MOUNTAINSIDE VINEYARDS
(See Chateau Chevalier Winery)

Mountain View
(See Gemello Winery)

Mount Madonna
(See Emilio Guglielmo Winery)

Muscat de Frontignan
(See Moscato Canelli)

Muscatel
A rich, flavorful, sweet dessert wine made from Muscat grapes and having their unmistakable flavor and aroma. Its color ranges from golden or dark amber to red. While most Muscatel is made from the Muscat of Alexandria grape and is golden in color, several other varieties are used in California to make Muscatels of varying flavor.

Red Muscatel, Black Muscatel: Muscatels which are red or dark red and are sometimes made from black Muscat grapes. Black Muscat is produced only by Novitiate Wines.

Muscat de Frontignan, Muscat Canelli: Muscatel made from the Muscat Blanc variety of Muscat grapes. Both names refer to the same grape.

Must
Unfermented grape juice, with or without the skins and seeds.

N

NAPA COUNTY
(Northern Coast) Appellations: Carneros, Yountville, Oakville, Rutherford, Calistoga, Stags' Leap, Pritchard Hill, Mount Veeder, Spring Mountain, St. Helena.

Wines to look for: Alatera, Alta Vineyard, Beckett, Beaulieu, Beringer, Burgess, Cakebread, Cassayre-Forni, Caymus, Chappellet Vineyard, Chateau Chevalier, Chateau Montelena, Christian Brothers, Clos du Val, Conn Creek, Cuvaison, Diamond Creek, Duckhorn Winery, Domaine Chandon, Flora Springs, Franciscan, Freemark Abbey, Grgich Hills, Heitz, Hanns Kornell, Inglenook Vineyards, Robert Keenan, Charles Krug, Long, Markham, Louis M. Martini, Mayacamas, Mont La Salle, Mt. Veeder, Robert Mondavi, Napa Vintners, Napa Wine Cellars, Nichelini, Niebaum-Coppola, Robert Pecota, Joseph Phelps, Pope Valley, Raymond, River Bend, Round Hill, Rutherford Hill, Rutherford Vintners, V. Sattui, Schramsberg, Charles Shaw, Silver Oak, Spring Mountain, St. Clement, St. Helena, Schramsberg Winery, Stags' Leap, Stags' Leap Wine Cellars, Smith-Madrone Stags' Vineyards, Sterling, Stonegate, Stony Hill, Sutter Home, Trefethen, Tulocay Winery, Villa Mt. Eden, Vose Vineyards.

NAPA, SOLANO

Napa Deluxe
  (See Matthews Napa Valley Winery)
Napa Gamay
  (See Gamay)
NAPA VALLEY COOPERATIVE WINERY
  P.O. Box 272, St. Helena, CA 04574
  Napa County
  Founded 1934. Winemaker is Dave M. Perez; Vineyard, 28 acres. Primarily provides quality wines to E & J Gallo.

NAPA VINTNERS

Box 2502, 17210 Action Ave. E, Napa, CA 95558
Napa County

Founded 1978. Owner and Winemaker is Don Charles Ross. Grapes are purchased on selected district basis from Napa and Lake counties.

100% varietal wines produced are Cabernet Sauvignon, Zinfandel, Chardonnay and Sauvignon Blanc (dry).

Winemaker's farovite wine is Sauvignon Blanc (dry).

NAPA WINE CELLARS

7481 St. Helena Hwy., Oakville, CA 94562
Napa County

Owner, Charles Woods; Vineyards, 30 acres.

NAPA CREEK VINEYARDS

3520 Silverado Trail North, St. Helena, CA 94574

NAVARRO VINEYARDS

5601 Hwy. 128, Philo, CA 95466
Mendocino County

Founded 1975. Owners are Ted Bennett and Deborah Cahn. The Winemaker is Edward Bennett. Vineyards are in Anderson Valley. Grapes are also purchased on a select vineyard basis.

Varietal, vintage-dated, Estate-bottled wines produced are Pinot Noir and Gewurztraminer.

Varietal, vintage-dated wines produced are Chardonnay, White Riesling and Cabernet Sauvignon. Also produced are Vin Rouge, Edelzwicker and Oeil de Perdrix.

Nebbiolo

(Red Table Wine) A varietal grape producing a dry, fruity and tart wine. Originally from Italy where it is used to produce Barolo and Gattinara.

NICASIO VINEYARDS

14300 Nicasio Way, Soquel, CA 95073
Santa Cruz County

Owner and Winemaker is Dan Wheeler, Grapes are purchased on a selected vineyard district basis.

Varietal, vintage-dated wines produced under the "Wines by Wheeler" label are White Riesling, Chardonnay, Zinfandel Rosé, Zinfandel and Cabernet Sauvignon. Brand "Wine by Wheeler". Also produced is Champagne (Natural).

NICHELINI VINEYARD

2349 Lower Chiles Road, St. Helena, CA 94574
Napa County

Founded 1980. Owner and Winemaker is Jim Nichelini. Established in 1890 by Anton and Catrina Nichelini and still carried on by grandson, Jim. Vineyard is east of Rutherford.

Varietal wines produced are Petite Sirah, Chenin Blanc, Sauvignon Vert, Cabernet Sauvignon, Semillon and Zinfandel.

The Winemaker's favorite wines are Petite Sirah and Chenin Blanc.

NIEBAUM-COPPOLA ESTATE

1460 Niebaum Lane, Rutherford, CA 94573
Napa County   (continued)

Founded 1978. Owner is Francis Ford Coppola; Wine-maker is Russ Turner; Vineyards, 110 acres.

Premium red table wine (blend of Cabernet Sauvignon, Cabernet Franc and Merlot). First release—Spring 1984, vintage 1978.

NERVO WINERY

19550 Geyserville Ave, Geyserville, CA 95441

Sonoma County

(Now owned by Geyser Peak)

Noble Rot

(See Botrytis)

NOBLE VINEYARDS

P. O. Box 31, Kerman, CA 93630

Kern County

Founded 1973. Owner, Pacific Land & Viticulture; Wine-maker, Richard de los Reyes; Vineyards, 3000 acres.

Varietal wines produced are French Colombard, Chenin Blanc, Semillon, Emerald Riesling, Ruby Cabernet and Barbera. Also produced are Dry White and Dry Red.

A. NONINI WINERY

2640 Dickenson Ave., Fresno, CA 93711

Fresno County

Founded 1935. Owner is Reno A. Nonini. Winemakers are Reno and Thomas Nonini; Vineyards, 200 acres.

Wines produced are red and white table wines.

Non vintage

Wines blended from several vintages in order to obtain a wine of higher quality. The purpose of this blending is to maintain consistency of quality and taste from year to year, without change in color, character, bouquet, etc.

NORDMAN OF CALIFORNIA

4836 E. Olive Avenue, Fresno, CA 93727

Founded 1972. President, James W. Hansen. Bulk wine only.

Nouveau

Literally "New" wine. In the tradition of Beaujolais, wine is bottled and released in late November, a few days after fermentation is finished. It is fresh, yeasty; with a hint of carbonation. Usually made from Gamay. Look for: Giumarra, Monterey Vyd., Pecota, Sebastiani. For Zinfandel Nouveau look for: Beringer or Franciscan.

NOVITIATE WINES

300 College Avenue, Los Gatos, CA 95030

Santa Clara County

Founded 1888. Owner of the winery is the Society of Jesus. The Winemaker is Brother Lee Williams, S. J. The vineyards are located at the winery in the foothills of the Santa Cruz Mountains.

The Estate-bottled wines are Dry Sauterne, Chablis, Chateau Novitiate (Haut Sauterne), Pinot Blanc, Chenin Blanc, Johannisberg Riesling (limited bottling), Grenache Rose, Pinot Noir (limited bottling), Ruby Cabernet, Dry, Cocktail and Flor Sherry. Black Muscat (unique), Tinta Port, Novitiate Angelica and Muscat Frontignan. The largest producer of Sacramental wines.

The Winemaker's favorite is Black Muscat.

Nutty

Term denoting the characteristic flavor of Sherry; not desirable in table wines.

O

OAK BARREL

1201 University Ave., Berkeley, CA 94702

Alameda County

Owner is Ivo Gardella. Winemaker is John Bank. Leaving Hungary in 1956 where he was a winemaker, John Bank started the winery in 1959. Grapes are purchased on a select vineyard basis from Napa and Sonoma Counties.

The varietal wines produced are Moscato Secco, Pinot Noir, Zinfandel and Cabernet Sauvignon. Also produced are Chateau Oak Barrel (White Wine), Light Muscat, Chablis and Vino Bianco. Sells wine in Bulk for parties and home bottling.

OAK GLEN WINERY

P.O. Box 381, Yucaipa, CA 92399

Founded 1977. Owners, Charles Colby, Frank Rivers; Winemaker, Charles Colby. Table Wine, fruit and berry wines.

OBESTER WINERY

Route 1, Box 20, Half Moon Bay, CA 94019

San Mateo County

Founded 1977. The Owners are Paul and Sandy Obester. The Winemaker is Paul Obester. Grapes are purchased on a select vineyard basis.

Varietal, vintage-dated wines produced are Sauvignon Blanc, Johannisberg Riesling, Cabernet Sauvignon and Zinfandel.

The Winemaker's favorite wine is the Sauvignon Blanc.

Oeil de Perdrix

A pale wine made from the free-run juice of Pinot Noir grapes. The French translation is "eye of the partridge." The same color as the bird's pink iris. Look for: Sebastiani, Navarro.

OLD GUASTI

(See Brookside)

OLD RANCH

(See Thomas Vineyards)

OLD ROSE

(See Bisceglia Bros.)

Oloroso

A sweet Sherry of medium type, darker and richer than Amontillado.

OPICI WINERY

Highland & Hermosa Ave., Alta Loma, CA 91701

Riverside County

Founded 1944. Owners, Mary Opici Nimmergut and Kurt Nimmergut. Produce table and sparkling wines.

Oreon

(See Gibson Winery)

Oxidation

The effect of air upon wine. The character of a wine can be substantially altered in proportion to its exposure to air. Partially filled bottles will quickly oxidize if not refrigerated. White wines not carefully made or stored will take on a brownish color and "burnt sugar" taste. The production of Sherry and Madiera requires slow oxidation.

P

PACHECO RANCH WINERY

5495 Redwood Hwy, Ignacio, CA 94947

Marin County

The Owner is the Rowland Family. The Winemaker is Jamie Neves. The vineyard is located at the winery. Winery on original Mexican land grant of Pacheo/Rowland family. The only winery producing from grapes grown in Marin County.

Varietal, vintage-dated wines produced are Cabernet Rosé and Cabernet Sauvignon.

PAGE MILL WINERY

13686 Page Mill Road, Los Altos Hills, CA 94022

Santa Clara County

Founded 1976. Owners are Richard and Alison Stark. Winemaker is Richard Stark. Vineyard, 1 acre. Grapes are purchased from growers on a selected district basis.

Varietal, vintage dated wines produced are Napa Valley Cabernet Sauvignon, Paso Robles Cabernet Sauvignon, Napa Valley Zinfandel, Paso Robles Zinfandel, Chenin Blanc (Santa Cruz Mountains), Napa Valley and Monterey Chardonnay and Livermore Valley Chardonnay. Also produced is Page Mill White (Rieslings).

Paisano

(See E & J Gallo)

Palomino

(Aperitif wine) The varietal grape produces a Sherry that is rather dry. Dominant Sherry grape grown in Central Valley area.

Panache

Aperitif. (See Domaine Chandon)

PANNONIA WINERY

3103 Silverado Trail, Napa, CA 94558

Napa County

Co-Owner and Winemaker is Dr. John D. Nemeth. Pannonia's name comes from a province of the Roman Empire. It is a beautiful hilly land now known as Western Hungary. Vineyards are located at the winery.

100% varietal, Estate-bottled, vintage-dated wines produced are Pinot Noir, Chardonnay and Sauvignon Blanc.

PAPAGNI VINEYARDS

31754 Avenue 9, Madera, CA 93637

Madera County

Founded 1973. The Owner is Angelo Papagni. The Winemaker is John Daddino. Founded by Demetrio Papagni who was a wine grape grower in Bari, Italy and came to California as a young man in 1912. In 1920, he planted his first 20 acres in the San Joaquin Valley. In the 1940's, Angelo planted vineyards in Madera County.

The varietal, vintage-dated, Estate-bottled wines produced are Chenin Blanc, Muscat Alexandra, Moscato D'Angelo, Late Harvest Emerald Riesling, Chardonnay, Dry Chenin Blanc (100%), Fumé Blanc, Alicante Bouschet, Barbera, Zinfandel, Charbono, Chardonnay Au Naturel, Sparkling Chenin Blanc and Gamay Rosé.

Also produced are Bianca Di Madera (Estate Bottled), Spumante D'Angelo (Estate Bottled), Brut Champagne, Extra Dry Champagne, Madera Rosé (Estate Bottled) and Sherry.

The Winemaker's favorite wines are Alicante Bouschet, Sparkling Chenin Blanc and Chardonnay.

Paradise
(See Bisceglia Bros.)

PARDUCCI WINE CELLARS
501 Parducci Rd., Ukiah, CA 95482

Mendocino County

Founded 1931. Owner is the Parducci family. The Winemakers are John Parducci and Joe Monostori. The vineyards are located in Ukiah. Founded in 1931, a third generation of Parducci's now work at the winery.

Varietal, vintage-dated wines produced are Gamay Beaujolais, Zinfandel, Carignane, Petite Sirah, Pinot Noir, Cabernet Sauvignon, Chenin Blanc, French Colombard, Mendocino Riesling, Chardonnay.

The Winemaker's favorite wines are French Colombard and Chardonnay.

PARSONS CREEK WINERY
3001 S. State St., Ukiah, CA 95482

Mendocino County

The Owners are Jess Tidwell and Hal Doran. Jess Tidwell is the Winemaker. Grapes are purchased on a select vineyard basis.

Varietal, vintage-dated wines produced are Chardonnay, Gewurztraminer and Johannisberg Riesling.

MICHAEL T. PARSONS WINERY
170 Hidden Valley Road, Soquel, CA 95073

Santa Cruz County

Founded 1976. Owner and Winemaker is Michael T. Parsons. Vineyards located in Santa Cruz Mountains and Santa Clara County.

Varietal, vintage dated wines produced are Cabernet Sauvignon and Pinot Noir.

PASTORI WINERY
23189 Geyserville Ave., Cloverdale, CA 95425

Sonoma County

Founded 1914. Owner, Frank Pastori; Vineyard, 60 acres.

PEACOCK HILL
(See Mark West Vineyards)

ROBERT PECOTA WINERY
3299 Bennett Lane, Calistoga, CA 94515   *(continued)*

Napa County

Founded 1978. Owner and Winemaker is Robert Pecota. Vineyard is at foot of Mt. St. Helena at end of Napa Valley.

Varietal, vintage-dated estate-bottled wines produced are Cabernet Sauvignon, Sauvignon Blanc and Gamay.

PEDRIZETTI WINERY

1645 San Pedro Ave., Morgan Hill, CA 95037

Santa Clara County

Founded 1938. The Owners are Ed, Phyliss and Dan Pedrizetti. The Winemaker is Ed Pedrizetti. Founded in 1938, the winery is now operated by three generations of the family.

Varietal, vintage-dated wines produced are Shell Creek Petite Sirah, Barbera, Petite Sirah, Cabernet Sauvignon, Zinfandel, Zinfandel Rosé, French Colombard, Chenin Blanc, Gewurztraminer, Pinot Chardonnay, White Barbera and White Zinfandel. Also produced are California Red and White.

Pedro Ximinez

(Dessert Wine) A varietal grape; produces a sweet dessert Sherry. Limited plantings in Central San Joaquin Valley.

J. PEDRONCELLI WINERY

1220 Canyon Road, Geyserville, CA 9544

Sonoma County

The Owners are John and James Pedroncelli. The Winemaker is John Pedroncelli. The winery was founded in 1904 and acquired by John Sr. in 1927. It is now owned and operated and by his sons. Vineyards are located at the winery and in Dry Creek Valley. Grapes are also purchased on a select vineyard basis in the Alexander and Dry Creek Valleys.

100% varietal, vintage-dated wines produced are Zinfandel Rosé, Gamay Beaujolais, Zinfandel, Cabernet Sauvignon, Johannisberg Riesling, Gewurztraminer, Chenin Blanc, French Colombard and Pinot Chardonnay. Also produced is the varietal, vintage-dated Pinot Noir. Two jug wines, Sonoma Red and Sonoma White, are produced.

PELLEGRINI BROS. WINERY

4055 West Olivet Rd., Santa Rosa, CA 95401

Sonoma County

Founded 1934. Owned by Pellegrini Wine Distributors, South San Francisco. Produces a unique "Clos du Merle". A field blend of Zinfandel, Petite Sirah, Cabernet Sauvignon and Gamay from hillside vineyard planted during the 1930s.

PENDLETON WINERY

2156-G O'Toole Avenue, San Jose, CA 95131

Santa Clara County

Founded 1977 as Arroyo Wines. The Owner and Winemaker is R. Brian Pendleton. Grapes are purchased on a selected region basis. Although relatively new, Pendleton has won several medals at competitive tastings.

Varietal, vintage-dated wines produced are Monterey Johannisberg Riesling, Monterey Chenin Blanc, Monterey Pinot Noir, Cabernet Sauvignon, Monterey Chardonnay, Livermore Valley Zinfandel, Monterey Select Harvest Johannisberg Riesling, Sonoma Sauvignon Blanc, Monterey Dry Chenin Blanc, Monterey Pinot Noir and Rutherford Cabernet Sauvignon.

PERELLI-MINETTI WINERY

Pond Road & Hwy. 99, Delano, CA 93216
Kern County
Founded 1933. Owner is the Perelli-Minetti family. (Also known as California Wine Association) The Winemaker is George Kolarovich. The vineyards are located at the winery. The vineyards were planted by Antonio Perelli-Minetti who was active in the winery until he was 94 years old. He was known for his viticultural expertise.

The Pereilli-Minetti label varietal, vintage-dated wines are Napa Valley Cabernet Sauvignon, Napa Valley Zinfandel, Monterey County Fumé Blanc, Napa Valley Chardonnay and Santa Clara County Johannisberg Riesling.

Under the Guasti Ambassador and Greystone labels are vintage-dated, varietal Cabernet Sauvignon, Zinfandel, Colombard Rosé, Chenin Blanc and French Colombard.

Vintage-dated generic wines are Burgundy, Chianti, Vin Rosé, Chablis, Sauterne, Rhine, Brut, Extra Dry and Pink Champagne, Cold Duck and Spumante. Also produced are Port, Pale Dry Sherry, Cream Sherry, Sherry and Marsala.

PESENTI WINERY

2900 Vineyard Drive, Templeton, CA 93465
San Luis Obispo County
Founded 1934. The Owner is the Pesenti family. The Winemakers are Frank Nerelli and Steve Pesenti. The Vineyard was first planted in 1923 and winery was founded in 1934 by Frank Pesenti.

Varietal, wines produced are Zinfandel, Zinfandel Blanc, Rosé of Ruby Cabernet, Ruby Cabernet, Zinfandel Rosé and Cabernet Sauvignon Blanc.

The Winemaker's favorite wines are Zinfandel and Zinfandel Blanc.

Pétillant

Slightly sparkling.

Petite Sirah

(Red Table Wine) A varietal grape that produces a dry, full-bodied, tannic wine. Believed to originate in the Middle East as the shiraz grape prior to being planted in France. The California Sirah is more of the French Duriff and is not the same as the famous Rhone Valley grape. Ages well. Excellent for big and well seasoned meals.

Look for: Assumption Abbey (Brookside), Barengo, Burgess, David Bruce, Caneros Creek, Callaway, Caymus, Concannon, Davis Bynum Dry Creek, Fieldstone, Fetzer, Freemark Abbey, Foppiano, Kenwood, J. Lohr, Llords & Elwood, Monterey Vineyards, Monterey Peninsula, Robert Mondavi, Mirrasou, Mt. Veeder, Novitiate, Pedrizzetti, Parducci, Joseph Phelps, Ridge, Roudon-Smith, Sonoma Vineyards, San Martin, Souverain, Stags' Leap Vineyards,

Petri

(See United Vintners)

JOSEPH PHELPS VINEYARDS

200 Taplin Road, St. Helena, CA 94574

Napa County

Founded 1973. Vineyards, 157 acres. Owner is Joseph F. Phelps. The Winemaker is Walter Schug. Vineyards are located at the winery. Grapes are also purchased from growers in Napa, Sonoma and Alexander Valley.

Varietal, vintage dated wines produced under the "Joseph Phelps Vineyard" label are Chardonnay, Sauvignon Blanc, Johannisberg Riesling, Gewurztraminer, Cabernet Sauvignon, Pinot Noir, Zinfandel and Petite Sirah.

Wines produced under the "Le Fleuron" label are Merlot, Cabernet Sauvignon, Vin Blanc and Vin Rouge.

Phenols

(See Tannin)

PICKLE CANYON VINEYARD

Mt. Veeder Road, Napa, CA

PINE RIDGE

5901 Silverado Trail, Napa, CA 94558

Napa County

The Owners are Gary Andrus and Mike Klassen; Winemaker, Tom Cottrell. The vineyard is located at the winery in the Stag's Leap region.

Varietal, vintage-dated wines produced are Cabernet Sauvignon and Chardonnay.

Pink Champagne

Pinot Noir or another dark-skinned grape is used to make the base wine. The pink color results from letting the juice remain with the grape skins during fermentation until the desired hue is obtained.

Pinot Blanc

(White Table Wine) A varietal grape that produces a light, dry, medium-bodied, moderately tart wine with a pronounced grape flavor and aroma. The better ones are rich and full and age well for 2–3 years.

Look for: Congress Springs, Chalone, Chateau St. Jean, Fetzer, Heitz, Inglenook, J. Lohr. Monterey Peninsula, Mirrasou, Roudon Smith, Wente Bros..

Pinot Chardonnay

(See Chardonnay)

Pineau de la Loire

(Christian Brothers Special Chenin Blanc)

Pinot Noir

(Red Table Wine) A varietal grape that produces clear, brilliant medium to deep red color. Rich, with just a hint of violets, velvety and full of flavor. Originally from France where it is used in all of the great red Burgundies: Beaune, Pommard and Cote D'Or. Serve with beef, lamb, fowl, veal and egg dishes. Also with fruit, nuts and cheese: Brie, Cheddar, Munster. Age 3 to 7 years.

Look for: Beaulieu, Beringer, Burgess, David Bruce, Deloach (Estate Bottled), Caymus, Richard Carey, Carneros

Creek, Clos du Bois, Chalone, Christian Bros., Daniele, Dehlinger, Fetzer (Special Reserve), Firestone (Vintage Reserve), Freemark Abbey, Foppiano, Gemello, Gundlach-Bundschu, Grand Crus, Hanzell, Hoffman Mountain Ranch, Haciena Wine Cellars, Husch, J.W. Morris, Keenan, Kenwood, Lawrence, Llords & Elwood, J. Lohr, Louis Martini, Paul Masson, Mt. Eden, Mirassou, Matanzas, Monterey Vineyards, Robert Mondavi, Novitiate, Pannomia (Estate Bottled), Pedroncelli, Parducci, Pendleton (Monterey), Martin Ray, Raymond, River Oaks, Rutherford Hill, San Martin, Sanford & Benedict, Simi, Spring Mountain, Joseph Swan, Souverain, Villa Mt. Eden, Weibel (North Coast), Z-D (Caneros).

Pinot Noir Blanc

White wine made from Pinot Noir grapes by removing juice from skins immediately after grapes are crushed.

Look for Caymus, Chateau St. Jean, Mark-West, Franciscan, Edmeades (Opal), Weibel, Mill Creek.

Pinot St. George

(Red Dinner Wine) A varietal grape that produces a robust, earthy, fruity wine similar to the California Gamay. A good accompaniment to red meats. Relatively rare.

Look for: Christian Bros.

PIPER-SONOMA

Windsor, CA 95492

Sonoma County

Joint venture founded 1980 to produce French style premium champagne in Sonoma County.

The Owners are French based Piper-Heidsieck and Renfield Importers. The Winemakers are Rodney D. Strong of Sonoma and Michel La Croix, Piper-Heidsieck's winemaster.

Varietal, vintage dated, bottle fermented (Method Champanoise) sparkling wines produced will be Brut, Blanc de Noir and a tete de cuvee.

PIRRONE WINE CELLARS

Pirrone Road, Salida, CA

Stanislaus County

Owner, Alfred F. Pirone; Vineyards, 425 acres.

L. POCAI & SONS

Rt. #1 Box 231, Calistoga, CA 94515

Napa County

Founded 1912.

Pomace

The pulp, skins and seeds of grapes remaining after the juice or newly fermented wine has been drawn off or pressed out.

POMMERAIE VINEYARDS

10541 Cherry Ridge Road, Sebastopol, CA 95472

Sonoma County

Owners and Winemakers are Ken and Arlene Dalton and Bob and Nora Wiltermood. The vineyards are located in Sonoma County.

Varietal, vintage-dated wines produced are Cabernet Sauvignon and Chardonnay. Also produced is a blend of Riesling and Gewurztraminer.

POPE VALLEY WINERY

6613 Pope Valley Road, Pope Valley, CA 94567
Napa County

Founded 1972. The Owner is the James M. Devitt Family. The Winemaker is Steve Devitt. Founded in 1909 by Ed Haus, a German Blacksmith, he built what was known as the "Burgundy Winery." When the Devitts purchased the property in 1972, it needed total restoration and they have been successful at retaining the natural beauty of the winery. Grapes are purchased on a select vineyard basis.

Varietal, vintage-dated wines produced are Napa County Chardonnay, Sonoma County Chardonnay, Dry Sauvignon Blanc, Dry Chenin Blanc, Johannisberg Riesling, Napa County Cabernet Sauvignon, Lake County Cabernet Sauvignon, Napa County Zinfandel, Sonoma County Zinfandel, Lake County Zinfandel, Napa County Petite Sirah and Lake County Petite Sirah.

The Winemaker's favorite wines are Chardonnay, Cabernet Sauvignon and Zinfandel.

PHILIP POSSON

(See Sierra Wine Co.)

Port

Port is a fortified, rich, fruity, heavy bodied, sweet wine, usually deep red. However, there is a lighter-colored, lighter-bodied Port called Tawny Port, and also a white Port which is straw colored. Port originated in Portugal. Many grape varieties can be used in making Port, including Carignane, Petite Sirah, Tinta Cao, Tinta Madeira and Zinfandel. Port is not baked (as Madera and some Sherries), influenced by yeast (as 'Flor' Sherry), nor flavored as Marsala. The alcohol content is usually 18–21%.

Look for: Christian Brothers (Tinta Cream), Ficklin, East Side (Tinta Madera), Llords & Elwood (Ancient Proverb), Paul Masson, J.W. Morris (Vintage), Quady (Vintage), Italian Swiss Colony, Wine & The People (Zinfandel Port), Woodbury Winery (Vintage), Richert and Sons.

POUR LE GOURMET

(See Louis Cherpin Winery)

Pourriture Noble

A state overripeness which concentrates the sugar content of grapes (See Botrytis).

PRAGER WINERY & PORT WORKS

1281 Lowelling Lane, St. Helena, CA 94574
Napa County

PRESTIGE VINEYARDS

48980 Seminole Drive, Cabazon,CA 92230
Napa County

Owners, Paul and Peggy Hadley.

PRESTON VINEYARDS

9282 West Dry Creek Road, Healdsburg, CA 95448
Sonoma County

Founded 1975. Owner and Winemaker is Louis D. Preston; Vineyards, 80 acres in Dry Creek Valley.

Varietal, vintage dated, estate-bottled wines produced

are Sauvignon Blanc, Zinfandel, Chenin Blanc, and Cabernet Sauvignon.

PRIDE OF CALIFORNIA
(See California Wine Co.)

PRIVATE CELLAR STOCK
(See James Frasinetti's & Sons)

Purchasing Wine—Store or Restaurant
The following are pointers to look for in a store or restaurant:

Name of producer.

Special labeling—indicating limited bottling, cask number, special reserve, etc.

Geographic origin—North Coast, Napa, Sonoma, etc. (Keep in mind that to indicate this, 75% of the grapes must come from that region.)

Vintage—to indicate a date means that 95% of the wine must be harvested and fermented in the year shown.

Estate-bottled—the grapes were grown and crushed on the estate of the winery and it was also bottled at the winery.

Q

QUADY WINERY
13181 Road 2Y, Madera, CA 93637
Madera County
Founded 1977. Owner and Winemaker is Andrew Quady. The vineyard is located in Amador County.

The wines produced are Amador County Zinfandel Port, Vintage Port Paso Robles and Zinfandel Ports in various types.

QUAIL RIDGE
3520 Silverado Trail, St. Helena, CA 94574
Napa County
Founded 1978. Owners and winemakers are Jesse and Elaine Corello. Vineyard is on Mt. Veeder Road. Varietal, vintage dated Chardonnay not yet released.

R

Racking
The drawing of wine from a storage cask into a fresh cask.

A. RAFANELLI
4685 West Dry Creek Road, Healdsburg, CA 95448
Sonoma County
Founded 1974. Owner and Winemaker is Americo Rafanelli. Vineyard is in Dry Creek Valley. Wines produced are Franken Riesling, Johannisberg Riesling, Cabernet Sauvignon and Cabernet Sauvignon Blanc (Grapes are picked at night to minimize red pigment extraction from the skins.)

RANCHITA OAKS WINERY
Estrella Rt., San Miguel, CA
San Luis Obispo County
The Owners are Ron Bergstrom and John Scott. The Winemaker is John Scott.

Varietal wines produced are Cabernet Sauvignon, Petite Sirah, Zinfandel and White Zinfandel.

RANCHO SISQUOC WINERY
Rt. 1, Santa Maria, CA 93454
Santa Barbara County
The Owner is James Flood. The Winemaker is Harold Pfeiffer. Vineyard is in Santa Maria Valley.

Varietal, vintage dated, Estate-Bottled wines produced are Franken Riesling, Johannisberg Riesling, Cabernet Sauvignon and Cabernet Sauvignon Blanc.

RAPAZZINI WINERY
4350 N. Monterey Hwy, Gilroy, CA 95020
Santa Clara County
(Also known as B&R Vineyards)
The Owners and Winemakers are Jon and Sandra Rapazzini. Founded in 1962 by Jon and father Angelo representing four generations of winemakers starting from Milano, Ilay. Grapes are purchased on a select vineyard basis.

100% varietal, vintage-dated wines produced are Gewurztraminer, Petite Sirah, Barbera, Fine Family Reserve Cabernet Sauveginon and Johannisberg Riesling.

The Winemaker's favorite wine is San Luis Obispo Johannisberg Riesling.

MARTIN RAY VINEYARDS
22000 Mt. Eden Road, Saratoga, CA 95070
Santa Clara County
Owner and Winemaker is Peter Martin Ray. Son of the late winemaker of the same name, the winery was founded in 1943. Grapes are purchased on a select vineyard basis.

100% Varietal, vintage dated wines produced are Pinot Noir, Chardonnay and Cabernet Sauvignon and Merlot. Methode Champenoise Champagne is also produced.

RAYMOND VINEYARD & CELLAR
849 Zinfandel Lane, St. Helena, CA 94574
Napa County
Founded 1974. Owners are Roy Raymond, Jr. and Sr. and Walter Raymond. The family has been involved in viticulture since the 1870's. Vineyard is in the Napa Valley.

Varietal, vintage dated wines produced are Napa Valley Cabernet Sauvignon, Gamay Merlot. Zinfandel, Pinot Noir, Chardonnay, Johannisberg Riesling, and Chenin Blanc. (Frequent medal winners)

Red Pinot
(See Pinot St. George)

Red Rock Terrace
(See Diamond Creek Vineyards)

Red Table Wines
Dinner or table wines are usually dry, suited to accompany main course dishes. Dry means most or all of the

grape sugar was fermented out, and thus the opposite of dry is sweet. Most red dinner wines are dry. Some red dinner wines are soft and mellow (i.e. slightly sweet) while others impart a robust astringence which results from tannin, the same substance that in tea makes your mouth slightly puckery. Most red dinner wines fall into two general types, Burgundy and Claret. There are also some semi-sweet red dinner wines sometimes known as "mellow red wines," or Vino Rossos. Alcohol content is from 10.5 to 14 percent, usually about 12 percent by volume. Red Dinner Wines—Generic: Burgundy, Claret, Chianti, Vino Rosso. Red Table Wines—Varietal: Barbera, Cabernet Franc, Cabernet Sauvignon, Charbono, Gamay (Napa Gamay), Gamay Beaujolais, Grenache, Grignolino, Merlot, Petite Sirah, Pinot Noir, Pinot Red (Pinot St. George), Ruby Cabernet, Zinfandel.

REDWOOD VALLEY CELLARS
(See Weibel Champagne Vineyards)

A. REGE WINE CO
26700 Dutcher Creek Road, Cloverdale, CA 95425
Founded 1939. Owner and Winemaker, Eugene Rege; Vineyards, 117 acres.

Rhine Wine
A white dinner or table wine, thoroughly dry, pleasantly tart, pale golden or slightly green gold in color. Medium bodied, fresh and fruity. Good with white meats and seafood.

RICHERT& SONS WINERY
18980 Monterey Road, Morgan Hill, CA 95037
Santa Clara County
The winery was founded in 1954 by Walter F. Richert. The Winemaker is Scott Richert.

Wines produced are primarily Sherry and Port. Recently has begun producing Alexander Valley Cabernet Sauvignon and Triple Cream Sherry.

RIDGE VINEYARDS
17100 Monte Bello Road, Cupertino, CA 95014
Santa Clara County
Founded 1962. The founding Owners are the Bennions, Cranes, Rosens along with Paul Draper and others. The Winemaker is Paul Draper. The vineyard is on the Monte Bello Ridge of the Santa Cruz mountains. Grapes from other areas are also used. If so, they are indicated on the back label.

Varietal wines produced are Petite Sirah, York Creek, Zinfandel, Late Harvest 1 (Shenandoah Valley, Amador County), Cabernet Sauvignon, York Creek; Ruby Cabernet, Monte Bello; Zinfandel, Late Harvest, Geyserville; Zinfandel, Paso Robles; Zinfandel, Jimsomare; Cabernet Sauvignon, Monte Bello; Zinfandel, Fiddletown; Zinfandel, San Luis II; Zinfandel, Coast Range III.

The Winemaker's favorites are the Cabernet Sauvignons, Petite Sirah and the mountain grown Zinfandels.

Ripe
The term used to describe a wine which has attained maturity, mellowness, perfection. When the term "ripe

for bottling ? " is used, it means the wine has improved in the cask to the highest point possible, after which again usually is completed in glass.

Ripple
(See E & J Gallo)

RITCHIE CREEK VINEYARDS
4024 Spring Mountain Rd., St. Helena, CA 94574
Napa County
Founded 1974. Owner, R. P. Minor; Vineyards, 4 acres at Spring Mountain. Varietal, vintage dated Cabernet Sauvignon is produced.

RIVERBEND WINERY
8643 Silverado Trail, Rutherford, CA 94573
Napa County
The Owners and Winemakers are Richard and Susan Shown. The vineyards are located at the winery.

Varietal, vintage-dated, Estate-bottled wines produced are Johannisberg Riesling, Zinfandel, Cabernet Sauvignon and Chenin Blanc.

RIVER OAKS VINEYARDS
Lytton Station Road, Healdsburg, CA 9544
Sonoma County
Owner is River Oaks Vineyard Corp. Winemaker is Paul Brasset. Vineyards are located in Alexander Valley.

Varietal wines produced are Chardonnay, Zinfandel, Pinot Noir, Pinot Noir Blanc, Gamay Beaujolais, Johannisberg Rielsing and Cabernet Suavignon. Also produced are soft Zinfandel (an aperitif wine), Zinfandel Rosé, Pinot Noir Rosé, Premium White Table Wine (1.5 liter, French Colombard and Sauvignon Vert), Premium Red Table Wine. Both table wines produced from Alexander Valley Vineyards.

RIVER ROAD VINEYARDS
6109 Anderson Rd, Forestville, CA 95436
Sonoma County
President, Gary Mills; Vineyards, 120 acres.

RIVER RUN VINTNERS
65 Rogge Lane, Watsonville, CA 95076
Santa Cruz County
Founded 1978. The Owners are Terra and William Hangen. William is the Winemaker. Vineyards, 4 acres. Grapes are purchased for their specific vineyard and regional characteristics.

Wines produced are Zinfandel (Morgan Hill), White Riesling (Ventana Vineyards), Pinot Noir (Ventana Vineyards), Zinfandel (Shandon Valley), Zin "Blush."

Winemaker's favorites are "Morgan Hill" Zinfandel and "Ventana Vineyards" Pinot Noir.

RIVERSIDE COUNTY
(Southern California) Wines to look for: Brookside, Callaway, Cilurzo and Piconi, Galleano Winery, Glen Oak Hills, Mount Palomar, Opici.

Rkatsiteli
(White Table Wine) A varietal grape of Russian origin producing a crisp, tart flavored wine with a delicate per-

fume. Only produced by Concannon. Serve with mild cheese and fresh fruit. Made only by Concannon.

RIVERSIDE, SAN BERNARDINO, SAN DIEGO

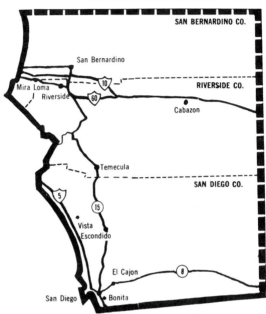

RODDIS CELLARS

1510 Diamond Mtn., Rd., Calistoga, CA 94515
Napa County
The Owner and Winemaker is William H. Roddis. The vineyard is on Diamond Mountain in Napa. Only wine produced is Varietal, vintage dated, Estate-Bottled Cabernet Sauvignon.

Roma

(See Guild Wineries)

Rosa

(See Sebastiani Vineyards)

Rosé

A pink dinner wine, sometimes called a luncheon wine. Rosé's range from dry to slightly sweet and are usually fruity-flavored light-bodied and made from Cabernet, Gamay, Grenache, Grignolino or Zinfandel grapes. Alcohol content is 10 to 14 percent, usually about 12 percent by volume. The pink or pale red color is obtained by removing the grape skins as soon as the required amount of color has been attained by the wine.

Rosé, Varietal table wines: Cabernet Sauvignon Rosé, Gamay Rosé, Grenache Rosé, Grignolino Rosé, Petite Sirah Rosé, Pinot Noir Rosé, Zinfandel Rosé. *(continued)*

Look for: Almaden (Grenache), Beaulieu, Brookside (Rosé of Cabernet), Caymus Oeil de Perdrix, Concannon (Zinfandel), Casa de Fruita (Zinfandel), Chappellet (Gamay), Christian Bros. La Salle, Dry Creek (Cabernet Sauvignon), Franciscan (Pinot Noir Blanc), Gallo (Grenache), Heitz (Grignolino), Johnson's Alexander Valley (Pinot Noir), Llords & Elwood (Cabernet), Marik West (Pinot Noir Blanc) , Mill Cr-ek (Cabernet Blush) Blush, Monterey Vineyard Classic, Robert Mondavi (Gamay), Sebastiani (Gewurztraminer), Sebastiani Eye of the Swan, Simi (Cabernet Sauvignon), Sonoma (Grenache), Ventana (Cabernet Sauvignon).

ROSENBLUM CELLARS
1775 Sixteenth St., Oakland, CA 94612
Alameda County
The Owners and Winemakers are the Rosenblums and the Hawleys. Grapes are purchased on a select vineyard basis from Mendocino, Sonoma and Napa Counties.

Varietal, vintage-dated wines produced are Pinot Chardonnay, Johannisberg Riesling, White Zinfandel, Gewurztraminer, Petite Sirah and Zinfandel.

The Winemaker's favorite wine is Johannisberg Riesling.

CARLO ROSSI
(See E & J Gallo)

Rotta
(See Las Tablas Winery)

ROUDON-SMITH VINEYARDS
2364 Bean Creek Road, Santa Cruz, CA 95065
Santa Cruz County
Founded 1972. Owners are Robert Roudin and James Smith. Winemaker is Robert Roudin. Vineyard is located in Santa Cruz County.

Varietal, vintage dated wines produced are Zinfandel, Chardonnay, Cabernet Sauvignon, Gewurztraminer, Pinot Blanc and Petite Syrah. Also produced is a sparkling wine.

Favorite wine of Winemaker is vintage Zinfandel.

ROUNDHILL CELLARS
1097 Lodi Lane, St. Helena, CA 94574
Napa County
Founded 1977. The Owners are Charles A. Abela and Max G. Sperling. The Winemaker is Doug Manning. Grapes are purchased on a selected vineyard basis.

Varietal, vintage-dated wines produced are Napa Chardonnay, Sonoma County Chardonnay, North Coast Chardonnay, Johannisberg Riesling, Napa Gewurztraminer, Napa Cabernet Sauvignon, Napa Valley Cabernet Sauvignon, North Coast Pinot Noir, Napa Zinfandel, Napa Valley Petite Sirah, Napa Gemay, Napa Valley Gamay Deaujolais and Napa Gamay Rosé.

Also produced are Chablis, Burgundy and non-vintage North Coast Cabernet Sauvignon.

Royal Host
(See East-Side Winery)

Royalty

A varietal grape that was developed at University of California to grow in San Joaquin Valley as a base for Port-type wines.

RUBEDOUX WINERY

3477 Arlington Avenue, Riberside, CA 92506
Owners, Joe Tavaglione and Sons.

Ruby

A port of very deep-red color, usually quite young, as opposed to one which has been aged for some time in wood and has become "tawny" which is pale in color through repeated tinigs.

Ruby Cabernet

(Red Table Wine) A varietal grape developed by the University of California to grow under the warm conditions of the San Joaquin Valley. It is the child of the Cabernet Sauvignon and the Carignane. The wine is dry, a Cabernet-like arome with good acidity and a fruity flavor. A red meat wine. Look for: Ridge, Barengo, Italian Swiss Colony.

CHANNING RUDD CELLARS

2157 Clinton Avenue, Alameda, CA 94501
Alameda County
Owner and Winemaker is Channing Rudd.

Varietal, vintage dated wines produced are Chenin Blanc, Chardonnay, Zinfandel, Merlot, Petite Sirah and Cabernet Sauvignon. Also Zinfandel-Cabernet Port.

RUTHERFORD CELLARS

(See Rutherford Vintners)

RUTHERFORD HILL WINERY

Rutherford Hill Road, Rutherford, CA 94573
Napa County
Founded 1976. Owner is a partnership. The managing partner is William Jaeger. The Winemaker is Phillip Baxter. The partnership also owns Freemark Abbey Winery. The vineyards are in Napa County.

The varietal, Estate-bottled, vintage-dated wines produced are Cabernet Sauvignon, Zinfandel, Merlot, Pinot Noir, Chardonnay, Johannisberg Riesling, Dry White Riesling, Gewurztraminer, Pinot Noir Blanc and Pinot Noir Nouveau.

RUTHERFORD VINTNERS

1673 St. Helena Hwy. South, Rutherford, CA 94573
Napa County
Founded 1977. The Owners are Bernard L. Skoda and a group of his friends. Bernard Skoda is the Winemaker. Established in 1976 after Skoda retired from Louis M. Martini. The vineyard is located at winery in Napa Valley.

Varietal, vintage-dated wines produced are Cabernet Sauvignon, Johannisberg Riesling and Pinot Noir.

Varietal, non-vintage Muscat of Alexandria is also produced.

The Winemaker's favorite wines are Cabernet Sauvignon and Johannisberg Riesling.

S

SACRAMENTO COUNTY

(Northern San Joaquin Valley) James Frasinetti & Sons, Gibson Wine Co.

SAN ANTONIO WINERY

737 Lamar St., Los Angeles, CA 90031

Founded 1917. Owner, the Riboli family. Several tasting rooms in Los Angeles area.

SAN BENITO COUNTY

(Central Coast—Inland) Appellations: Paicines. Wines to look for: Almaden, Calera, Casa De Fruta, Cygnet, Enz, San Benito Vineyards.

SAN BENITO VINEYARDS

251 Hillcrest Road, Hollister, CA 95023

San Benito County

Founded 1970. Winery is owned by Dr. Rodney, Sandra and Robert Ballard. The Winemakers are Robert and Rodney Ballard. Wines produced are pure fruit and berry—Apricot, Pomegranate, Strawberry, Bing Cherry, Plum, Pear, Peach, Blackberry and Raspberry.

The Winemaker's favorites are Apricot and Pomegranate.

SAN BERNARDINO COUNTY

Southern California) Brookside Winery, Guasti, J. Filippi Vintage, Louis Cherpin, Thomas Vineyards.

SAN DIEGO COUNTY

Appellations: Rancho California and Temecula.

Wines to look for: Bernardo, Brookside, Ferrara, J. Filippi, San Pasqual.

SANFORD AND BENEDICT VINEYARDS

Santa Rosa Road, Lompoc, CA 93436

Santa Barbara County

The Owners and Winemakers are Richard Sanford and Michael Benedict. The vineyard is located at the winery.

Varietal, vintage-dated Estate-Bottled wines produced are Pinot Noir, Chardonnay, Cabernet Sauvignon, Merlot and Riesling.

Sangrole

(See United Vintners)

SAN JOAQUIN COUNTY

Barengo Vineyards, Cadlolo Winery, California Cellar Masters (Coloma), Delicato Vineyards, Eastside Winery, Franzia Brothers, E & J Gallo, Liberty Winery, Lucas Homes Wines, Turner Winery.

SAN JUAN BAUTISTA

(See B & R Vineyards)

SAN LUIS OBISPO COUNTY

(Central Coast) Appellations: Paso Robles.

Wines to look for: Estrella River, Hoffman Mountain Ranch, Lawrence, Las Tablas, Mastantuono, Pesenti, York Mountain.

SAN MARTIN WINERY

P.O. Box 53, San Martin, CA 95046

Santa Clara County   *(continued)*

Owner is Somerset Wine Co., a division of Norton Simon, Inc. The Winemaker is Ed Friedrich. Grapes are purchased on a selected vineyard basis in Santa Barbara, San Luis Obispo, Monterey, Santa Clara and Amador Counties.

Vintage-dated, varietal wines produced are Pinot Chardonnay, Fumé Blanc, Johannisberg Riesling, Emerald Riesling, Chenin Blanc, Gewurztraminer, Muscat di Canelli, Malvasia Bianca, Semillon, Zinfandel Rosé, Cabernet Sauvignon Rosé, Gamay Beaujolais, Pinot Noir, Cabernet Sauvignon, Zinfandel and Petite Sirah.

Under the label of San Martin, the soft wines (low alcohol 7–10%) the varietal, vintage-dated wines produced are Soft Chenin Blanc, Soft Johannisberg Riesling, Soft Gamay Beaujolais and Soft Zinfandel. The vintage-dated table wines are Chablis, Rhine, Rosé and Burgundy. Also produced is Montonico (a dessert wine similar to Sherry).

Winemaker's most interesting wine is the Soft Johannisberg Riesling which was pioneered as the first California table wine released with less than 10% alcohol.

SAN JOAQUIN, STANISLAUS

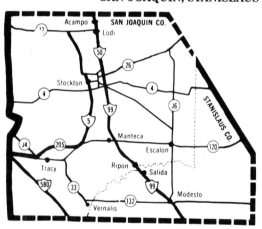

SAN PASQUAL VINEYARDS
13455 San Pasqual Road, Escondido, CA 92025
San Diego County
Founded 1973. The general partners are Charles Froehlich and Milton Fredman. The Winemaker is Kerry Damskey. The vineyard is in the San Pasqual Valley.

The varietal, vintage-dated wines produced are Chenin Blanc (100%), Sauvignon Blanc (100%), Muscat Canelli (100%) and Napa Gamay Rosé (100%). Also produced are a NV Fumé Blanc, Vintage Gamay and NV San Pasqual Red.

The Winemakers favorite wines are Gamay and Fumé Glanc.

SAN MATEO COUNTY

(San Francisco Bay—Central Coast) Wines to look for: Obester Winery, Sherrill Cellars.

SANTA BARBARA COUNTY

(South Central Coast) Appellations: Santa Maria and Santa Ynez.

Wines to look for: J. Carey Cellars, Firestone Vineyard, Rancho Sisquoc, Sanford and Benedict, San Martin, Santa Barbara, Santa Ynez Valley, Zaca Mesa Winery.

SAN LUIS OBISPO, SANTA BARBARA, VENTURA

SANTA BARBARA WINERY

202 Anacapa Street, Santa Barbara, CA 93101
Santa Barbara County
Founded 1972. The Owner is a California Corporation. The winery was started by Pierre LaFond who is the Winemaker. The vineyard is in the Santa Ynez Valley.

Wines produced are a 100% varietal Chenin Blanc plus a Chablis. Fruit wines are produced under the Solvang label.

SANTA CLARA COUNTY

(Central Coast) Appellations: Santa Clara Valley, Canta Cruz Mountains and Gilroy-Hecker Pass.

Wines to look for: Almaden, Bertero, Brookside, David Bruce, Casa de Fruta, Congress Springs, Fortino, Gemello, E. Guglielmo, Hecker Pass, Kathryn Kennedy, Kirigin, Thomas Kruse, La Purisima, Ronald Lamb, Live Oaks, Llords and Elwood, Martin Ray, Paul Masson, Pendleton, Mirrassou, Mount Eden, Novitiate, Page Mill, Pedrizzetti, Rapazzini's, Richert and Sons, San Martin, Sarahs Vineyard, Sherrill, Sommelier, Sycamore Creek, Turgeon and Lohr.

SANTA CRUZ CELLARS

(See Bargetto's)

SANTA CRUZ COUNTY

(Central Coast) Wines to look for: Ahlgren, Bargetto's, Devlin Wine Cellars, Felton-Empire, Frick Winery, Michael T. Parsons, River Run, Roudon-Smith, Santa Cruz Mountain, P & M Staiger, Sunrise.

SANTA CRUZ MOUNTAIN VINEYARD

2300 Jarvis Road, Santa Cruz, CA 95065
Santa Cruz County
Founded 1975. Owner and Winemaker is Ken D. Durnap. Vineyard, 12 acres. Vineyard is located at the winery.

Varietal wines produced are Pinot Noir and Cabernet Sauvignon.

Santa Fe

(See United Vintners)

SANTA YNEZ VALLEY WINERY

365 North Refugio Road, Santa Ynez, CA 93460
Santa Barbara County
Founded 1976. Owners are the Bettencourt, Davidge and Brander families. The Winemaker is C. Frederic Brander. The vineyards are in the valley which is 35 north of Santa Barbara. A young but already medal-winning winery.

The estate-bottled, 100% varietal, vintage-dated wines produced are Sauvignon Blanc, Semillon Chardonnay, Chardonnay Reserve de Cave (sold only at winery), Blanc de Cabernet Sauvignon, White Riesling, Merlot, Cabernet Sauvignon and Gewurztraminer.

The Winemaker's favorites are the Sauvignon Blanc and the Chardonnay Reserve de Cave.

SANTINO WINERY

Steiner Road, Plymouth, CA
Amador County
The owners are Matthew and Nancy Santino. The winemaker is Scott Harvey. Grapes are purchased on a select vineyard basis. Varietal wines produced are White Zinfandel, Zinfandel and Cabernet Sauvignon.

SARAH'S VINEYARD

4005 Hecker Pass Hwy. Gilroy, CA 95020
Owners, Otteman Berry, Hicks, McManigal and R. Vallalobos; Vineyards, 7 acres. Varietal wines produced are Chenin Blanc, Chardonnay, Zinfandel, Petite Sirah, Grenache red and Grenache white.

V. SATTUI WINERY

White Lane, St. Helena, CA 94574
Napa County
The Owner and Winemaker is Daryl Sattui. Daryl is the great-grandson of the original owner Vittorio who started the winery in 1885. The vineyard is 2 miles south of St. Helena. Grapes are also purchased on a select vineyard basis.

Vintage-dated, varietal wines produced are Cabernet Sauvignon (Napa Valley), Zinfandel (Amador County), Pinot Blanc, Johannisberg Riesling (Dry) and (Napa Valley). A vintage-dated Burgundy is also produced. Excellent cheese & gift shop and picnic area at the winery.

SAUSAL WINERY
7370 Hwy. 128, Healdsburg, CA 95448
Sonoma County
The Owners are David, Edward and Roselee Demostene and Lucinda Nelson. The Winemaker is David Demostene. Vineyards are in the Alexander Valley and at winery. The Demostene family has a long history of winemaking in Alexander Valley.

Varietal, vintage-dated Estate-bottled wines produced are Zinfandel, Cabernet Sauvignon, Pinot Noir Blanc and Chardonnay. Also produced is Sausal Blanc.

Sauterne
Sauterne wines are golden-hued, fragrant, full-bodied, white dinner or table wines ranging from dry to sweet. In California, there are three types of Sauterne—Dry Sauterne, Sauterne, and Sweet, Haut or Chateau-type Sauterne. They vary greatly because the sweetness of the three Sauterne types is not defined by regulations. Generally, California Sauternes are drier than those of France. Sauvignon, Blanc and Semillon are predominant varietals and are discussed under their individual names. Generic Sauterne is traditionally a blend of Semillon, Sauvignon Blanc and Muscadelle du Bordelais.

Sauvignon Blanc
(White Table Wine) A varietal grape producing a white table wine that ranges from dry to sweet. When produced "dry", the wine is excellent with seafood and poultry. When sweet it is delightful to sip after being well chilled. Also a good accompaniment for cake and fresh fruit.

One of the principal grapes of the Sauterne district of France. The Sauvignon Blanc also has several aliases using the Fumé name before or after the Blanc. Fumé Blanc, Blanc Fumé/Sauvignon and Blanc de Sauvignon. The wines carrying the Fumé tend to be drier with a grassy or smoky taste. Sauvignon Blanc is richer, sweeter and fruitier unless indicated as "dry".

Look for: Almaden, Callaway—Temecula Fumé, Cakebread, Chateau St. Jean—Sonoma Fumé, Christian Bros.—Napa Fumé, Concannon, Dry Creek—Sonoma Fumé, Estrella River, Foppiano, E & J Gallo, Geyser Peak—Sonoma Fumé, Lawrence, Obester, Preston, Paul Masson Pinnacles, Robert Mondavi Napa Fumé, Montevina, Napa Vintners, Papagni, Joseph Phelps, Parducci, San Pasqual, Santa Ynez Valley, Sterling, Souverain, Spring Mountain, Stonegate, Sutter Home.

Sauvignon Vert
A varietal grape that is mainly used for blending because of its high acidity. Not a true Sauvignon.

SCHRAMSBERG VINEYARDS
Calistoga, CA 94515
Napa County
Founded 1862. The managing director is Jack Davies. The Winemaker is Harold Osborne. Established in 1862 by Jacob Schram, this was the first winery on the hillsides of the Napa Valley. The vineyards are located at the winery. Designated as a Historical Landmark in 1957, Robert Louis Stevenson wrote of Schramsberg in

his "Silverado Squatters" when he visited in 1880.

Champagnes produced are bottle fermented Reserve, Blanc de Blanc, Blanc de Noirs, Cuveé de Pinot and Crémant.

SEBASTIANI VINEYARDS

389 Fourth Street East, Sonoma, CA 95476

Sonoma County

Founded 1904. The Owner is the Sebastiani Family. Winemakers are Jim Carter and Doug Davies. The original vineyard was founded in 1825 by the Padres of the Mission de Sonoma. It was the first vineyard north of San Francisco. In 1904 Samuel Sebastiani bought the vineyard and started the winery.

Vintage-dated, varietal wines produced as "Proprietor's Reserve" are Zinfandel, Barbera and Pinot Noir. Vintage-dated, varietal wine produced under the "Rosa" label is Gewurztraminer.

Vintage-dated, varietal wines produced are Sylvaner Riesling, Pinot Noir Blanc "Eye of the Swan," Pinot Chardonnay, Green Hungarian, Johannisberg Riesling, Gewurztraminer, Chenin Blanc, Mountain French Colombard, Mountain Chenin Blanc, Nouveau Gamay Beaujolais (when available), Gamay Beaujolais, Pinot Noir, Zinfandel, Cabernet Sauvignon, Barbera, Mountain Cabernet Sauvignon, Mountain Pinot Noir, Mountain Zinfandel.

Also produced are Vin Rosé, Grenache Rosé, Mountain Vin Rosé, Chablis, Mountain Chablis, Chianti, Burgundy, Mountain Burgundy, Arenas Dry Sherry, Amore Cream Sherry and Adagio Tawny Port.

Sec

French word for "dry". Usually applied to Champagne it actually means medium sweet.

Sediment

The solids which are contained in a wine. They do not signify that a wine is not drinkable, rather sometimes prove that it has perfected itself in the bottle.

SEGHESIO WINERY

P.O. Box 24035—Redwood Highway, Cloverdale, CA 95425

Founded 1902. Owners, Eugene and Edward Seghesio; Vineyards, 300 acres.

Sémillon

(White Table Wine) A varietal grape that is a companion to the Sauvignon Blanc in the Sauternes region of France. The wine is made in both a dry and sweet version. Dry it has a perfumey, aromatic flavor. Goes well with poultry and cream sauces. Sweet it is rich and full. Good to sip or with desserts.

Look for: Santa Ynez, Stony Hill, Matanzas, Wente Bros., Barengo and Valley of the Moon.

Serving temperatures

Champagne: 50°; Red Table wine: 65°–70°; Sherry: 65°–70° ; Port: 65°–70°; Rosé: 50°; White Table Wine: 55°.

SEQUOIA CELLARS

1110 Lincoln Ave., Woodland, CA 95695   *(continued)*

Yolo County

Owners and Winemakers are Carol Gehrmann and Patricia Riley. Varietal wines produced are Carnelian, Gewurztraminer, Zinfandel and Cabernet Sauvignon.

ROBERT SETRAKIAN VINEYARDS

P.O. Box 21, Yettem, CA 93670

Tulare County

The Owner is the Setrakian Family. The Winemaker is Robert Setrakian. Founded in 1906 by Arpaxat "Sox" Setrakian. Vineyards are located at winery.

Varietal, vintage dated wines produced are Cabernet Sauvignon, Petite Sirah, Grenache Rosé, Chenin Blanc, French Colombard, Emerald Riesling and Johannisberg Riesling. Also produced are Blanc de Blanc Brut Champagne, Sherry and Port.

SHAFER VINEYARDS

6154 Silverado Trail, Napa, CA 94558

Owners, John and Elizabeth Shafer; the Winemaker is Nikko Schoch. Vineyards, 40 acres in Stag's Leap region. Varietal, vintage dated wines produced are Chardonnay, Cabernet Sauvignon and Zinfandel.

CHARLES F. SHAW VINEYARD & WINERY

1010 Big Tree Road, St. Helena, CA 94574

Napa County

Owner and Winemaker is Charles "Chuck" Shaw.

Varietal, vintage-dated wine produced is Napa Gamay.

SHENANDOAH VINEYARDS

Box 23 Steiner Road, Plymouth, CA 95669

Amador County

Owners are Leon and Shirley Sobon. The Winemaker is Leon Sobon. Vineyards are located in the Shenandoah Valley. Grapes are also purchased on a select vineyard basis.

Varietal, vintage-dated wines produced are White Zinfandel, Chenin Blanc, Zinfandel, Cabernet Sauvignon, Late Harvest Zinfandel and Mission Del Sol.

The Winemaker's favorite wine is Cabernet Sauvignon.

Shermat

Short for "Sherry material." Young wine, adjusted by the addition of wine spirits to the desired alcohol content, destined to be made into Sherry by one of several different methods.

SHERRILL CELLARS

1185 Skyline Blvd., Woodside, CA 94062

Santa Clara County

Owners are Nathaniel and Jan Sherrill. The Winemaker is Nat Sherrill.

Vineyard being planted at winery location. Grapes purchased on a select vineyard basis.

Varietal, vintage dated wines produced are Cabernet Sauvignon, Zinfandel, Petite Sirah and Gamay. Under skyline label blended wines are produced.

Winemaker's favorite wines are Zinfandel and Petite Sirah.

Sherry California

The most popular appetizer wine of all, is often made

from Palomino, Mission or Pedro Ximenes. Sherry has a characteristic "nutty" flavor. Its color ranges from pale gold to dark amber, and it is either dry, medium dry or sweet. The sweet is often called "cream" sherry.

The sweeter Sherries are usually served with dessert, or between meals refreshment.

Look for: Christian Bros., E & J Gallo, Llords & Elwood, Brookside, S. Richert & Sons, Italian Swiss Colony.

Sherry, California Dry

Light straw to light amber in color with a nutty sherry character. Light in body, but mellow. Sugar content should be lower than 2.5%.

Sherry, California, Dry Flor & Medium Flor

Same characteristics and sugar content of corresponding sherries with the exception of a pronounced flor or mild yeasty flavor.

Sherry—California, making

Although many different grapes are used to make Sherry, in California, many winemakers use Mission, Palomino, Thompson Seedless and Pedro Ximenes. After fermentation of the juice has reached the desired stage— when the wine is as dry as the producers style requires— brandy is added to stop fermentation. The new wine is called shermat in the California wine industry. Then many wineries age the wine at a warm temperature in lined or stainless stell or concrete tanks or in redwood containers. This process, at temperatures anywhere between 100 to 140° F (38° to 60° C) continues from three months to a year. Sometimes it is done in a heated room, sometimes in tanks heated by coils, and sometimes by the heat of the sun. Later, the Sherry is allowed to cool gradually to cellar temperature and it is then aged like other wines. The heating, the oxidation due to the prolonged contact of the warm wine with air, and the aging in wood barrels all combine to develop the pleasant "nutty" flavor characteristic of California Sherry. In addition, other California wineries produce a "flor" Sherry, using either the Spanish method which allows a film— yeast growth called "flor" to form on the surface of the wine in partially-filled containers or the "submerged flor" process. These also impart a distinctive flavor to the wine. Some other wineries offer blends of baked and "flor" Sherries.

Some California wineries operate Sherry Soleras. A solera consists of barrels lying one on top of another four or five tiers high, the oldest at the bottom and the youngest at the top. At periodic intervals, the matured Sherry is drawn from the bottom barrel to be bottled. This barrel is then replensihed from the one above, and so on. The top barrel is filled with new wine. By this method the young wine mixes with the older to provide a uniform product of high quality year after year.

Sherry, California, Medium

Light golden amber to medium golden amber in color. Medium-bodied, nutty character. Sugar content should be between 2.5 and 4.0 %.

Sherry, California, Sweet (Cream)

Medium to dark amber in color. Full bodied, rich and nutty with well developed Sherry character. Sugar content should not be less than 4.0 %.

SHILO VINEYARDS

8075 Martinelli Rd., Forestville, CA 95436

Sonoma County

Owners are Jacob and Barbara Shilo. The Winemaker is Steve Test. The vineyard is located at the winery in the Russian River area.

Varietal, Estate-bottled wines produced are Pinot Noir, Cabernet Sauvignon, Riesling and Chardonnay.

SHOWN & SONS VINEYARD

8643 Silverado Trail, Rutherford, CA 94573

Napa County

The owners are Richard L. Shown and Gary Gouvea. The Winemaker is Tom Cottrell. Vineyards are in Rutherford.

Varietal, vintage dated wines produced are Cabernet Sauvignon, Zinfandel, Johannisberg Riesling and Chenin Blanc.

SIERRA VISTA WINERY

4560 Cabernet Way, Placerville, CA 95667

El Dorado County

Founded 1977. The Owners are John and Barbara MacCready. The Winemaker is John MacCready. Vineyard is located at the winery.

Varietal, vintage-dated wines produced are Zinfandel, Fumé Blanc, Cabernet Sauvignon and Rosé of Cabernet Sauvignon.

SIERRA WINE CO.

555 West Shaw Ave., Fresno, CA 93704

(209) 227-4067

Owner, Berge Kirkorian; Winemaker, Phil Posson. Primarily bulk wine.

SILVER MOUNTAIN

P.O. Box 1695, Los Gatos, CA 95030

Santa Cruz County

The Owner and Winemaker is Jerry O'Brien. Grapes are purchased on a select region basis.

Varietal, vintage-dated wine produced is Zinfandel.

SILVER OAK CELLARS

915 Oakville Cross Road, Oakville, CA 94562

Napa County

Owners are Justin R. Meyer and Raymond T. Duncan. Winemaker is Justin R. Meyer. Grapes are purchased on a selected district basis.

Varietal wine produced is Cabernet Sauvignon (aged five years).

SIMI WINERY

Box 946, Healdsburg, CA 95448

Sonoma County

The Owner is Moet-Hennessy as of Domain Chandon. Moet-Hennessy is the French company that also owns Champagne Moet & Chandon, Mercier and Ruinart, Hennessy Cognac and Dior Perfumes.   *(continued)*

Giuseppe Simi came to California in the years of the gold rush and for thirty years he tried his hand at mining and farming. When he and his brother Pietro first saw the green hills of the Alexander Valley and the nearby town of Healdsburg, they were struck by the resemblance to their native village. Here was the perfect place for a winery. In 1876 they created their own winery and carefully selected the finest grapes available. Andre Tchelistcheff, master enologist is consultant. Winemaker is Zelma Long.

Varietal, vintage-dated "North Coast" wine produced is Zinfandel.

Varietal, vintage dated "Alexander Valley" wines produced are Pinot Noir, Cabernet Sauvignon, Rosé of Cabernet Sauvignon, Chenin Blanc, Johannisberg Riesling, Gewurztraminer, Chardonnay and Gamay Beaujolais.

SKY VINEYARDS
4352 Cavedale Rd, Glen Ellen, CA 95442
Owners, Lore and Aleta Olds; Vineyards, 20 acres.

SKYLINE
(See Sherrill Cellars)

SMITH-MADRONE VINEYARDS
4022 Spring Mountain Road, St. Helena, CA 94574
Napa County
Founded 1977. Owner is the Cook's Flat Association. Winemaker is Stuart Smith. Vineyard is located near the winery.

Varietal wines produced are Chardonnay, Cabernet Sauvignon, Pinot Noir and Johannisberg Riesling.

SMOTHERS-VINE HILL WINES, INC.
2317 Vine Hill Road, Santa Cruz, CA 95065
Santa Cruz County
The Owner is R. R. Smothers (famous entertainer). The Winemaker is William Arnold. A relatively new winery that won the Grand Prize for its Gewurztraminer '77 in 1978 at the L.A. County Fair. The vineyard is located at the winery in Santa Cruz mountains. Grapes are also purchased on a selected vineyard district basis.

The 100% varietal, vintage-dated wines produced are Cabernet Sauvignon (Sonoma), Gewurztraminer (Sonoma), Zinfandel (San Luis Obispo), White Riesling (San Luis Obispo).The varietal, vintage-dated wines produced are White Riesling (Santa Cruz), Chardonnay (San Luis Obispo) and White Riesling.

SODAROCK WINERY
7370 Hwy 128, Healdburg, CA 95448
Owners, Rose Demostene, Renn Steele, Inez Nuessle, Vera Plu.

Soft Wines
New low alcohol, (7–10%), wines.

SOLANO COUNTY
(North Coast Inland from Napa) Wines to look for: Cadenasso, Diablo Vista, Wooden Valley.

Solera
The Spanish system of progressively blending Sherries

in tiers of small casks—to blend Sherries of the same type but varying ages.

SOMMELIER WINERY
2560 Wyandotte Street, Mountain View, CA 94043
Santa Clara County
Founded 1976. Owners are the Keezer and Burnham Families. The Winemaker is Richard C. Keezer. Grapes are purchased on a selected vineyard district basis.

Varietal wines produced are Zinfandel, Cabernet Sauvignon, Grenache Rosé, Ruby Cabernet, Petite Sirah and Pinot Noir.

SONOMA COUNTY
(North Coast) Appellations: Sonoma Valley, Russian River Valley, Alexander Valley, Dry Creek and Geyserville.

Wines to look for: Alexander Valley, Ballverne, Bandiera (New Arroyo Sonoma), Bellrose, Buena Vista Haraszthy, Davis-Bynum, Cambiaso, Chateau St. Jean, Clos du Bois, H. Coturri & Son, Dehlinger, Donna Maria Vineyard, Dry Creek, Field Stone, Fenton Acres, Foppiano, Frei Bros,, Geyser Peak, Grand Cru, Gundlach-Bundschu, Hacienda, Hanzell, J. J. Haraszthy, Hop Kiln, Horizon, Iron Horse, Italian Swiss, Johnson's Alexander Valley, Jordan, Kenwood, Korbel Champagne Cellars, La Crema, Lambert Bridge, Landmark, Lytton Springs, Mark West, Matanzas Creek, Mill Creek, Nervo, Pastori, J. Padroncelli, Pellegrini, A. Rafanelli, Rege, Sausal, Sebastiani, Shilo, Simi, Soda Rock, Sonoma Vineyards, Sotoyome, Souverain, Joseph Swan, Robert STemmler, Russian River, Trentadue, Valley of the Moon, Vina Vista, Willowside.

SONOMA COUNTY CELLARS
P.O. Box 925, Healdsburg, CA 95448
Owner, F. M. Passalacqua.

SONOMA COUNTY COOPERATIVE WINERY
P.O. Box 36, Windsor, CA 95492
Founded1935. Under contract to E & J Gallo.

SONOMA VINEYARDS
Windsor, CA 95492
Sonoma County
Founded 1961. Ownership is a publicly held corporation. The Winemaker is Rodney D. Strong who was the original founder and who also selected the seven locations and planted the vineyards in Sonoma County.

Varietal, vintage-dated wines produced are Cabernet Sauvignon, Chardonnay, Pinot Noir, Johannisberg Riesling, Petite Sirah, Zinfandel, Chenin Blanc, Grey Riesling, French Colombard, Ruby Cabernet, Grenache Rosé and Champagne.

Varietal, vintage-dated, Estate-bottled wines are produced only in exceptional years and are bottled in a special, gold-script label. They are Chardonnay, Johannisberg Riesling, Pinot Noir, Zinfandel and Cabernet Sauvignon. Other brands: Windsor vineyards and Tiburon Vintners.

The Winemaker's favorite wines are Alexanders

Crown Cabernet Sauvignon, River West and Chalk Hill Chardonnay.

SOTOYOME WINERY

641 Limerick Lane, Healdsburg, CA 95448

Sonoma County

Owner is C S Wines, Inc. The Winemaker is William Chaikin. Vineyards are located at winery and in Dry Creek Valley. Grapes are also purchased on a select vineyard basis.

Varietal, vintage-dated wines produced are Zinfandel, Petite Sirah, Cabernet Sauvignon and Chardonnay.

The Winemaker's favorite wine is Petite Sirah.

Sour

A sour wine is a spoiled wine. It is inaccurate to call a dry, astringent, or tart wine "sour".

SOUVERAIN

P.O.Box 528, Geyserville, CA 95441

Sonoma County

Founded 1943. Souverain is owned by over 240 growers of the North Coast Grape Growers Association, who are located in the counties of Napa, Sonoma and Mendocino. General Manager is Joe Vercelli. Bill Bonetti is the Winemaker. All wines are produced from 100% North Coast grapes. All carry a vintage label. The wines produced are Cabernet Sauvignon, Charbono, Pinot Noir Rosé, Chardonnay, Gewurztraminer, Johannisberg Riesling, Colombard Blanc, Grey Riesling, Dry Chenin Blanc, Fume Blanc, Merlot and Muscat Canelli. Recommend: Gewurztraminer and Petite Sirah.

Spanada

(See E & J Gallo)

Sparkling Burgundy

A red wine made sparkling by secondary fermentation in closed containers. It is usually semi-sweet or sweet. Barbera, Carignane, Petite Sirah and Pinot Noir are the grapes most used for its production.

Sparkling Wines

Sparkling wines are wines which have been made naturally effervescent by a second fermentation in closed containers. Sparkling wines can be red, pink or white, with an alcohol content of 10–14 percent.

Sparkling wines: Champagne Cold Duck, Sparkling Burgundy, Sparkling Muscat, Sparkling Rosé.

SPRING MOUNTAIN VINEYARDS

2805 Spring Mountain Road, St. Helena, CA 94574

Napa County

The Owners are Michael and Shirley Robbins. Sid Greenberg is a limited partner. The Winemaker is John Williams. Vineyard is located in the Napa Valley.

Varietal vintage-dated, Estate-bottled wines produced are Cabernet Sauvignon, Chardonnay, Sauvignon Blanc and Pinot Noir.

STAG'S LEAP WINE CELLARS

5766 Silverado Trail, Napa, CA 94558

Napa County

Owners are Barbara and Warren Winiarski. The Winemaker is Warren Winiarski. The Cabernet Sauvignon and Merlot vineyards are located in the Napa Valley. It was the 1973 Stag's Leap Cabernet Sauvignon that set the French on their ear in 1976 when it came in first in the Paris tasting. Mouton-Rothschild '70 was second.

Varietal, vintage-dated, Estate-Bottled wines produced are Cabernet Sauvignon and Merlot. Varietal, vintage dated wines produced are Cabernet Sauvignon (Napa Valley), Chardonnay (Haynes Vineyard) and (Napa Valley), Johannisberg Riesling (Birkmyer Vineyards) and (Napa Valley), Gamay Beaujolais (Napa Valley), Merlot (Napa Valley). Also produced under the Hawk Crest label is Cabernet Sauvignon and Johannisberg Riesling.

Winemaker's favorite wines are Stag's Leap Vineyards Cabernet Sauvignon and Haynes Vineyard Chardonnay.

STAGS' LEAP WINERY
6150 Silverado Trail, Napa, CA 94558
Napa County
(No connection with Stag's Leap Wine Cellars)

The Owners are Carl and Joanne Doumani. The vineyards are located at the winery.

Varietal wines produced are Chenin Blanc, Petite Sirah and Merlot.

The Winemaker's favorite wine is Petite Sirah.

P AND M STAIGER
1300 Hopkins Gulch Road, Boulder Creek, CA 95006
Santa Cruz County
Founded 1973. The Owners are Paul and Marjorie Staiger. The Winemaker is Paul Staiger. Original vineyard was planted in 1900. Replanted by the Staigers in 1973. Vineyard is at winery north of Boulder Creek at elevation of 1100 feet. Vineyard also in Templeton.

Varietal, vintage-dated wines produced are Chardonnay (Estate-bottled), Cabernet Sauvignon (Estate-Bottled) and Zinfandel.

ST. ANDREWS WINERY
2921 Silverado Trail, Napa, CA 94558

Stanford
(See Weibel Champagne Vineyards)

STANISLAUS COUNTY
(Central San Joaquin Valley) Wines to look for: Pirone Wine Cellars, JFJ Bronco, E & J Gallo.

ST. CLEMENT VINEYARDS
2867 St. Helena Hwy. North, St. Helena, CA 94574
Napa County
Founded 1975. Owners are Doctor William and Mrs. Alexandra Casey. The Winemaker is Chuck Ortman. The house that appears on the label is a Napa Valley landmark that was built in 1876 and it is in the cellars of this Victorian home that the first wines of Spring Mountain Vineyards were made. The Casey's purchased the property in 1975. The vineyards are located at the winery and in St. Helena, Rutherford and Yountville.

The varietal, vintage-dated wines produced are Chardonnay and Cabernet Sauvignon.

STEEN WINERY

Whitehall Lane, St. Helena, CA 94574

Napa County

The Owners are Alan and Charlene Steen. The Winemaker is Art Finkelstein.

Grapes are purchased on a selected vineyard basis from Alexander Valley.

Varietal, vintage-dated wines produced are Chardonnay, Cabernet Sauvignon and Sauvignon Blanc.

STEVENOT VINEYARDS

San Domingo Road, Murphys, CA 95247

Calaveras County

Founded 1978. Owner is Barden E. Stevenot. Winemakers are Barden E. Stevenot and Julia Iantosca. The vineyard is located at the winery. The varietal, vintage dated wines produced are Chenin Blanc (Northern California) (Calaveras County) Chardonnay, Zinfandel Blanc, White Riesling, Cabernet Sauvignon (Calaveras), Zinfandel (Calaveras).

Winemakers' favorite wine is Calaveras Chenin Blanc

ST. FRANCIS VINEYARDS

8450 Sonoma Hwy., Kenwood, CA 95452

Sonoma County

Owner, Joseph Martin. The Winemakers are Joseph Martin and Brad Webb. The vineyards are in the Sonoma Valley. Varietal, vintage dated, Estate-Bottled wines produced are Chardonnay, Gewurztraminer, Merlot, Pinot Noir and Johannisberg Riesling.

ST. HELENA WINE CO.

(DUCKHORN VINEYARDS)

3027 Silverado Trail, St. Helena, CA 94574

Napa County

Owner, Duckhorn Family; Winemaker, Thomas Rinaldi; Vineyards, 5 acres in Napa Valley. Varietal, vintage dated wines produced are Merlot, Cabernet Sauvignon and Sauvignon Blanc.

ROBERT STEMMLER WINERY

3805 Lambert Bridge Road, Healdsburg, CA 95448

Sonoma County

The Owners are Robert Stemmler and Trumbull W. Kelly. The Winemaker is Robert Stemmler, he was formerly winemaker at Charles Krug, Inglenook and Simi. Vineyard (Chardonnay) located at the winery. Grapes are also purchased on a select vineyard basis.

Varietal, vintage-dated wines produced are Fumé Blanc, Cabernet Sauvignon and Estate-bottled Chardonnay.

STERLING VINEYARDS

1111 Dunaweal Lane, Calistoga, CA 94515

Napa County

Founded 1964. The Owner is the Coca Cola Co. (The Wine Spectrum). The Winemaker is Theo Rosenbrand. The vineyards are located in the Napa Valley.

The varietal, vintage-dated, Estate-Bottled wines produced are Chardonnay, Sauvignon Blanc, Cabernet Sauvignon and Merlot. Still produced but will be eliminated in the early 1980's are Chenin Blanc, Cabernet Blanc,

Gewurztraminer, Pinot Noir and Zinfandel. Under the label "Sterling Reserve" a vintage-dated, Estate-Bottled Cabernet Sauvignon is produced.

The Winemaker's favorite wine is the "Reserve" Cabernet Suavignon.

STONEGATE WINERY

1183 Dunaweal Lane, Calistoga, CA 94515

Napa County

Owners are James C. and Barbara G. Spaulding. The Winemakers are David B. Spaulding and Michael Fallow. Winery has two vineyards. A hillside vineyard above the city of Calistoga at 800 feet and one located at the winery.

Wines produced are all varietal, vintage dated. Pinot Noir, Estate-bottled; Napa Cabernet (with Merlot for blending); Alexander Valley Cabernet; North Coast Chardonnay; Pinot Noir Blanc, Estate-Bottled; French Colombard, Estate-bottled; and Shasta County Sauvignon Blanc.

STONY HILL VINEYARD

P.O. Box 308, St. Helena, CA 94574

Napa County

Founded 1953. The Owner is Mrs. Frederick H. McCrea. The Winemaker is Michael A. Chelini. Owned by the McCreas since 1952. Mr. McCrea passed away in 1977. The vineyard is in the foothills north of St. Helena.

Varietal, vintage-dated, estate-bottled wines produced are Chardonnay, White Riesling, Gewurztraminer and Semillon de Soleil (A sweet dessert wine).

The Winemaker's favorite wine is Chardonnay.

STONERIDGE

Ridge Road East, Sutter Creek, CA

Amador County

Owners are Gary and Loretta Porteous. The vineyard is located at the winery.

Vintage-dated, estate-bottled varietal wines produced are Zinfandel, White Zinfandel and Ruby Cabernet.

STONY RIDGE WINERY

1188 Vineyard Ave., Pleasanton, CA 94566

Alameda County

The Owner is Harry Rosingana. The Winemaker is Bruce H. Rector. The vineyards are located at the winery in the Livermore Valley. The original Ruby Hill Winery was established in 1887. The Rosinganas changed the name when they restored the winery in 1975.

The varietal, vintage-dated, Estate-bottled wines produced are Gamay Blanc, Chardonnay, Zinfandel, Cabernet Sauvignon and Mavasia Bianca.

The Winemaker's favorite is the Chardonnay.

SOUTH COAST CELLARS

12901-B South Budlong Ave., Gardena, CA 90247

Owner and Winemaker is Douglas J. Anderson. Grapes are purchased on a selected vineyard district basis.

Varietal wines produced are Cabernet Sauvignon and Zinfandel.

Stop Fermentation

The term that describes how, in winemaking, a little

pure grape brandy is added to a sweet dessert wine to check the fermentation. This prevents complete conversion of the nautral grape sugar into wine alcohol and carbon dioxide so that the wine is sweeter than if fermentation had run its course. Never use the word "fortify" in connection with wine. It is unlawful, under federal regulations plus many States.

STORY VINEYARDS
1917 P. St., Sacramento, CA 95814
Owner, E. C. Story; Vineyards, 27 acres.

STORYBOOK MOUNTAIN VINEYARDS
3835 Hwy 128, Calistoga, CA 94515
Napa County
The owner and winemaker is Dr. J. Bernard Seps. The vineyard is in the Napa Valley. The varietal, vintage dated wine produced is Zinfandel.

Sugar Content
The following are average sugar percentage contents: Aperitif: 0.5 – 3.5 %; Red: 0 – 1.5 %; White: 0 – 4.0 %; Rosé: 0 –2.0%; Dessert: 5.0 – 14 %; Champagne: 0.5 – 5.0 %.

Note: Late Harvest White Wines might go from 4% to 6% or more.

Sugars
Ripe grapes have around 20% of their weight as sugar but this is changed into about 12% alcohol by the yeast during fermentation. About 0.2% in fully fermented (dry) wine analyzes out as reducing sugar. Supposition is that 0.2%, more or less, is made up of odd sugars that the yeast cannot handle. Normal threshold for sugar is around 0.5%. Sugar content is the main index of grape ripeness; normally the higher the sugar content (expressed as degrees Balling or Brix), the riper the grapes are.

In warm climate zones the sugar content of grapes tends to increase to high levels while the natural acidity, at the same time, drops to very low levels and eventually the wine quality is poor. In cool climate zones (California Coastal regions Monterey for example) the acidity remain high during ripening, even as the sugar content in the grapes build to optimum ripeness levels and the eventual quality of the wine can be outstanding.

SULLIVAN VINEYARDS WINERY
1090 Galleron Lane, Rutherford, CA 94573
Napa County
The Owners are James and JoAnn Sullivan. The Winemaker is James B. Sullivan. Varietal, vintage dated wines produced are Chenin Blanc, Chardonnay, Zinfandel and Cabernet Sauvignon.

Summit
(See Geyser Peak Winery)

SUNRISE WINERY
16001 Empire Grade Rd., Santa Cruz, CA 95060
Santa Cruz County
Owners are Keith Hohlfeldt, Rolayne and Ronald Stortz.

Winemaker is Keith Hohlfeldt. Vineyards are located in Santa Cruz Mountains.

Varietal wines produced are Pinot Noir, Zinfandel, Cabernet Sauvignon, Chardonnay and Chenin Blanc.

The Winemaker's favorite wines are the Cabernet Sauvignon and Pinot Noir.

SUTTER HOME WINERY

277 St. Helena Hwy. South St Helena, CA 94574
Napa County
Founded 1874. Owner of the winery is the Trinchero family. The Winemaker is Louis "Bob" Trinchero. The winery was originally built in 1874. The Trinchero's purchased it in 1946.

All grapes are purchased from Amador County and El Dorado County. The varietal wines produced are Amador County Zinfandel, El Dorado County Zinfandel, White Zinfandel and Moscato Amabile, 100% Muscat Alexandria.

The Winemaker's favorite wine is Amador County Zinfandel.

SWAN, JOSEPH VINEYARDS

2916 Laguna Rd., Forestville, CA 95436
Sonoma County
Founded 1969. Owners are Joseph A. and June Swan; Vineyards, 10 acres are in Sonoma at winery. Grapes are also purchased on a select vineyard basis.

Varietal, vintage dated wines produced are Chardonnay, Pinot Noir and Zinfandel.

T. J. SWANN

(See United Vintners)

SWEETWATER SPRINGS

(See Hop Kiln Winery)

SYCAMORE CREEK VINEYARDS

12775 Uras Road, Morgan Hill, CA 95037
Santa Clara County
Founded 1976. Owners are Walter and Mary Kaye Parks. The Winemaker is Walter Parks. Originally started in 1906 by the Marchetti family who came as settlers. The vineyard is located at the winery.

Varietal, vintage-dated wines produced are Cabernet Sauvignon, Chardonnay, Zinfandel and Carignane.

Sylvaner

(White Table Wine) A varietal grape that produces a semi-dry to just a touch of sweetness, soft, clean and fruity wine. Not a Riesling although sometimes labeled as Franken Riesling. Goes well with shellfish, poultry and light meats.

T

Table or dinner wine

The "right" name for all still wines with not over 14% Alcohol content by volume. Most table or dinner wines are dry, but it is wrong to call all of them "dry" wines.

That was formerly the practice but it has been discontinued because many dinner wines, like Sweet Sauterne, are actually semi-sweet or sweet, while some wines of the dessert or appetizer class, like Sherry, are nearly dry. "Table" or "dinner wine" is the "right" term because most wines of that class are used with meals and also because the term guides the consumer in selecting wines of this class for mealtime use. The class includes the wines sometimes referred to as "light wines," "dry wines," or natural wines.

Tannins or phenols

Give the wine its red color, astringent or bitter taste (but not "tart") and much of what the tongue senses as "body" in the wine.

Tannin in wine comes from grape skins, stems (even seeds if they happen to get crushed) but also, important to the eventual wine flavor, from barrels the wine was aged in at the winery. Most white wines are lower in tannin than most red wines, but no grape wine is completely free of it. However, white wines aged in wood (Chardonnay, Sauvignon Blanc and a few others) can contain lots of tannin, one of the reasons that these wines live longer in the bottle than others. Tannins are natural antioxidants and, since oxygen is the greatest enemy of aging wine, tannins are responsible for extending the life of bottled wine. "Fresh and Fruity" white wines, not aged in wood and not fermented in contact with skins or stems, don't contain much tannin and don't taste bitter or astringent and don't have long lives in the bottle.

Tart

Possessing agreeable acidity; in wine, tartness reflects the content of agreeable fruit acids.

Tasting Wine

In tasting wines the color, clarity, aroma, bouquet, tartness, flavor, astringency, degree of sweetness and balance are all to be considered

Look for judging color and clarity.

Smell for aroma and bouquet.

Taste for flavor.

Tavola

(See Guild Wineries)

Tawny

Wines having turned from red and brownish in color during maturation. Also a style of cask-matured Port.

TAYLOR CALIFORNIA CELLARS

(See The Monterey Vineyard) Wines labeled Taylor California Cellars are produced by Dr. Richard Peterson.

TEPUSQUET VINEYARD

Rt. 1, Santa Monica, CA 93454
Santa Barbara County

THOMAS VINEYARDS

8916 Foothill Blvd., Cucamonga, CA 91730
Los Angeles County

Founded 1839. The Owner is the Filippi family. The Winemaker is Joe Filippi, Jr. Designated as a historical landmark, on March 3, 1839, Tiburcio Tapia was given the Cucamonga land grant by Juan Alvarado, Governor of Mexico. Tapia built an adobe home, planted a vineyard and started California's first winery. Now owned by the Filippi family who started when Joseph and his father Giovanni came to America in 1922 to plant their first vineyard. Vineyard is located in Mira Loma.

Wines produced are Zinfandel, Grenache Rosé, Chablis, Blanc Rhine and Burgundy.

Thunderbird
(See E & J Gallo)

TIBURON VINTNERS
(See Sonoma Vineyards)

TOPOLOS at RUSSIAN RIVER WINERY
5700 Gravenstein Hwy, No. Forestville, CA 95436
Sonoma County
Owner, Michael Topolos; Vineyards, 110 acres.

TOROSA VINEYARDS
(See Richard Carey Winery)

Tokay
Tokay is midway in sweetness between Sherry and Port. It is amber-colored with a slightly "nutty" or Sherry-like flavor. It is a blend of dessert wines, usually Angelica, Port and Sherry. California Tokay is not to be confused with Tokay wines from Hungary or with the Flame Tokay grape, which may or may not be used in its production.

TRADER JOE'S WINERY
538 Mission St., South Pasadena, CA 91030
(Private labels Trader Joe's, Raymond Hill, Chateau Arroyo and Schloss Josef for own stores) Recently won a number of medals.

Traminer
(White Table Wine) A varietal grape that produces a light, fruity, semi-dry, soft wine. Originally from the Alsace province of France. Serve with shellfish and poultry.

TREFETHEN VINEYARDS
1160 Oak Knoll Ave., Napa, CA 94558
Napa County
Founded 1973. Owner is the Trefethen Family. The Winemaker is David Whitehouse, Jr. Founded in 1886 and known as "Eschol" ranch the owners won a first award for Cabernet Sauvignon at the San Francisco Viticultural Fair in 1880. The Trefethen family acquired the property in 1968. The vineyards are located in Napa.

The 100% varietal, vintage-dated, estate-bottled wines produced are Chardonnay, White Riesling, Pinot Noir and Cabernet Sauvignon (sometimes blended with Merlot).

Also produced are Eschol White wine and Eschol Red wine.

TRINITY WINE
Geyserville, CA
Sonoma County
The President is Al Carretta.   *(continued)*

Varietal, vintage-dated wines produced are Cabernet Sauvignon, Zinfandel, Johannisberg Riesling and French Colombard.

TRENTADUE WINERY

19170 Redwood Hwy., Geyserville, CA 95441
Sonoma County
Founded 1969. The Owner is Leo Trentadue. The Winemakers are Leo and Victor Trentadue. The vineyard is located at the winery in Sonoma County.

100% Varietal, vintage-dated, Estate-bottled wines produced are Semillon, Pinot Chardonnay, Johannisberg Riesling, French Colombard, Chenin Blanc, Zinfandel, Petite Sirah, Merlot, Gamay, Carignane, Cabernet Sauvignon and Aleatico. Also produced are Early Burgundy and Burgundy.

Winemaker's favorite wines are Petite Sirah and Zinfandel.

TUDAL WINERY

1015 Big Tree Road, St. Helena, CA 94574
Napa County
Owners, Arnold and Alma Tudal; the Winemaker is Charles Ortman. Vineyards, 10 acres in the Napa Valley. Varietal, vintage-dated, Estate Bottled wine produced is Cabernet Sauvignon.

TULOCAY WINERY

1426 Coombsville Road, Napa, CA 94558
Napa County
Founded 1975. Owners are William C. and Barbara Cadman. The Winemaker is William Cadman. Grapes are purchased from selected growers on a district basis.

100% varietal wines produced are Cabernet Sauvignon, Pinot Noir, Zinfandel and Chardonnay.

Favorite wine of Winemaker is Pinot Noir.

TULARE COUNTY

(San Joaquin Valley) California Growers

TUOLUMNE COUNTY

(Sierra Foothills) Yankee Hill Winery

TURGEON & LOHR WINERY / J LOHR WINES

1200 Lenzen Avenue, San Jose, CA 95126
Santa Clara and Monterey County
Founded 1974. The Owners are Bernard J. Turgeon and Jerome J. Lohr. The Winemaker is Peter M. Stern. The winery was converted from the historic Falstaff Brewery in San Jose. The vineyards are in Monterey County.

The varietal, vintage-dated wines produced are Chenin Blanc, Chardonnay, Johannisberg Riesling, Pinot Blanc, Cabernet Sauvignon Rosé, Monterey Gamay, Zinfandel, Petite Sirah, Cabernet Sauvignon, Sauvignon Blanc and Selected Clusters Chardonnay (Limited Bottling).

Also produced is Jade, a white wine.

The Winemaker's favorite wine is Monterey Gamay.

JOHNSON TURNBILL VINEYARD

8210 St. Helena Hwy., Oakville, CA 94562
Napa County
The Owners are Reverdy and Marta S. Johnson and

William Turnbill, Jr. The Winemaker is Reverdy Johnson. Vineyards are located in Napa Valley.

Varietal, vintage-dated, Estate-Bottled wine produced is Cabernet Sauvignon.

TURNER WINERY
3750 E. Woodbridge Rd., Acampo, CA 95220
Owner, the Turner Family; Winemaker, Peter Smiderle; Vineyards, 600 acres.

TYLAND VINEYARDS
2200 Mc Nab Ranch Road, Ukiah, CA 95482
Mendocino County
The Owners are Dick and Judy Tijsseling. The Winemaker is Dick Tijsseling. Vineyards, 250 acres. The vineyard is in Mendocino County.

Varietal, vintage-dated wines produced are Petite Sirah, Carignane, Cabernet Sauvignon and Zinfandel.

Tyrolia
(See E & J Gallo)

U

Ullage
The amount of air-space above a wine in a bottle or cask which is no longer full. Excessive ullage leads to spoilage.

UNITED VINTNERS INC.
601 4th St., San Francisco, CA 94107
Chairman of the Board, J. A. Powers; President, Robert A. Martin. Includes: Inglenook and Italian Swiss Colony Wineries.

Wineries located in Lodi, Madera, Escalon, Asti, Reedley, Rutherford, Oakville and Clovis California.

Wines range from vintage Inglenooks to pop wines such as Annie Green Springs. Brands include: Colony, Bali Hai, Lejon, Detri, Santa Fe, Jacques Bonet, Gambrello, T. J. Swann, Sangrole, HMS Frost, Jacare & Espirit.

Italian Swiss Winemaker Tom Eddy recommends their Cabernet Sauvignon, Ruby Cabernet, French Colombard, Crystal Chablis and Pale Dry Sherry.

Inglenook Winemaker Tom Farrell recommends the Charbono and Blanc de Noir.

URAS
(See Kirigin Cellars)

V

VACHE
(See Brookside)

VALLEY OF THE MOON WINERY
777 Madrone Road, Glen Ellen, CA 95442
Sonoma County
Founded 1944. The Owners are E & H Parducci. The Winemaker is Otto Toschi. The name Valley of the Moon

comes form the Wappo, Miwok and Pomo Indians. Originally "Valley of the Seven Moons," Jack London, the writer, shortened the name. Originally a portion of the Agua Caliente Rancho granted by the Mexican Government to Lazaro Pena, the land was purchased by General M.G. Vallejo. In 1851, Joseph Hooker took over 640 acres and planted a vineyard. He went on to become the famous "Fighting Joe Hooker" of the Union Army. These are the vineyards that surround the winery. Enrico Parducci bought the winery and vineyard in 1941.

The varietal, estate-bottled wines produced are Zinfandel, Zinfandel Rosé, French Colombard and Semillon. Also produced are Chablis, Burgundy, Claret and Vin Rosé.

Varietal

When a wine is named for the principal grape variety from which it is made it is said to have a varietal name. Cabernet Sauvignon, Chardonnay, Muscatel, Pinot Noir are some of the varietal names for wine types in the United States.

VEEDERCREST VINEYARDS

1401 Stanford Ave., Emeryville, CA 94608

Napa County Vineyards

Founded 1972. Managing Director and Winemaker is Alfred W. Baxter. The vineyard is on a crest of Mt. Veeder. Grapes are also purchased from selected Vineyards. Veedercrest has won many medals at competitive tastings.

Varietal, vintage-dated wines produced are Pinot Noir, from Sonoma County; Cabernet Sauvignon from Napa Valley, North Coast Counties and Alexander Valley; Cabernet Blanc from Alexander Valley; Chardonnay from Napa and Sonoma Counties; (Late Harvest) Gewurztraminer, Napa County; Pinot Noir Blanc, Sonoma County; Malbec from North Coast Counties and Napa County (Mt. Veeder District); Merlot, Napa County; White Riesling, (botrytis) Napa County; and Muscat of Alexandria.

VEGA VINEYARD WINERY

9496 Santa Rosa Road, Buellton, CA 93427

Santa Barbara County

The Owner and Winemaker is William M. Mosby. There is a vineyard three miles west of Buellton and vineyard located at the winery in the Santa Ynez Valley. Varietal, vintage dated wines produced are two styles of Riesling wines, a Johannisberg with 4% residual sugar, and White Riesling fermented dry. Also Gewurztraminer and Pinot Noir.

VENTANA VINEYARDS WINERY

P.O. Box G, Soledad, CA 93960

Monterey County

Founded 1978. The Owners are J. Douglas and Shirley Meador and Ralph Gonzales. The Winemaker is J. Douglas Meador. Vineyard is on Arroyo Seco River in Monterey County.

Varietal, vintage-dated wines produced are Chardonnay, Chenin Blanc (Dry), Pinot Blanc (Dry), White Riesling (Mosel Anish), Petite Sirah, Pinot Noir, Cabernet Sauvignon, Zinfandel "Summerwine," Gamay Beaujolais and Sauvignon Blanc (Dry and Botrytis).

Vermouth

A wine flavored with herbs and other aromatic substances. The two principal types are dry (pale) and sweet (dark) and usually fortified with Brandy.

For Vermouth, neutral white wines are first selected and aged. Then they are flavored by an infusion of herbs, and more aging follows. Vermouth ranges from 15–20 percent alcohol content.

NICHOLAS G. VERRY

400 First St., Parlier, CA 93684

Fresno County

Owner and Winemaker is John N. Verry. Specializes in Greek style resin flavored wines. Resin imported from Greece. Only current producer of Retsina in America.

CONRAD VIANO WINERY

150 Morello Ave., Martinez, CA 94553

Contra Costa County

VIEW'S LAND VINEYARD & WINERY

18701 Gehricke Rd., Sonoma, CA 95476

Sonoma County

The Owners are Walter Benson and Lu Williamson. The Winemaker is Lu Williamson. The vineyard is located at the winery and Cabernet is purchased.

Varietal, vintage-dated wines produced are Gewurztraminer, Chardonnay and Cabernet Sauvignon.

VIKINGS FOUR

(See Copenhagen Cellars)

VILLA ARMANDO WINERY

553 St. John St., Pleasanton, CA 94566

Alameda County

Founded 1903. Owner is the Scotto Family. Winemaker is Ed Chisholm. Vineyards are located near the winery. The Scotto's have been a winemaking family for over 100 years. Their wines are primarily distributed on the East Coast.

Wines produced are Rustico Red, Rustico Mellow Red, Rustico Mellow White, Rustico Mellow Pink Rosé, Burgundy, Barberone, Chianti, Rubinello, Orobianco, Zinfandel, Chablis, Malvasia Bianco, Burgundy (vintage), Zinfandel (vintage), Chablis (vintage), Pinot Noir, Orogianco, Cabernet Sauvignon and Champagne.

VILLA MT. EDEN

600 Oakville Crossroads, Oakville, CA 94562

Napa County

Founded 1974. The Owners are James K. and Anne McWilliams. The Winemaker is Nils Venge. The vineyards are located at the winery in the heart of the Napa Valley. Both vineyard and winery have existed since the early 1880s.

100% varietal, vintage-dated, Estate-bottled wines produced (all dry style) are Cabernet Sauvignon, Chenin Blanc, Pinot Chardonnay, Pinot Noir, Gewurztraminer and Napa Gamay.

VILLA BIANCHI WINERY
5806 N. Modoc Ave., Kerman, CA 93630
Kern County
Owner is Joseph Bianci. Vineyards are located near winery.

Varietal wines produced are Zinfandel, Grenache Rosé, Cabernet Sauvignon and French Colombard (Primarily bulk wines).

VINA VISTA VINEYARDS
Chianti Road, Geyserville, CA 95441
Sonoma County
Founded 1971. President, Keith Nelson.

VINE FLOW
(See Bella Napoli Winery)

THE VINEYARD
13180 Pièrce Road, Saratoga, CA
Santa Clara

VIN MONT
(See Napa Valley Cooperative Winery)

Vinosity
The grape character, and the effect of the wine's actual alcohol strength.

Vintage
The gathering of grapes and their fermentation into wine; also the crop of grapes or wine of one season. A vintage wine produced in the U.S. is one labeled with the year in which at least 95% of its grapes were gathered and crushed and the juice therefrom fermented. A vintage year is one in which grapes reach full maturity. Particularly applicable in Europe where growing conditions vary greatly from year to year. Less applicable in California where grapes reach maturity every year.

VOLCANIC HILL
(See Diamond Creek Vineyard)

VOSE VINEYARDS
4035 Mt. Veader Rd., Napa, CA 94558
Napa County
Owner and Winemaker is Hamilton Vose; Vineyards, 40 acres in Napa Valley. Varietal, vintage dated wines produced are Chardonnay, Cabernet Sauvignon, Fumé Blanc, Zinfandel and White Zinfandel.

W

WALKER WINES
25935 Estacada Dr., Los Altos, CA 94022
Santa Clara County
The Owners and Winemakers are Russ and Driz Walker. Grapes are purchased on a select region basis.

Varietal, vintage-dated wines produced are Chardonnay and Petite Sirah.

WEIBEL VINEYARDS
1250 Stanford Ave., Mission San Jose, CA 94538
Alameda County and Mendocino County
The Owner is Fred E. Weibel, Sr. The Winemaker is

Oscar Habluetzel. The vineyards are in the Santa Clara and Redwood Valleys. The vineyards date back to 1806 and the winery was established in 1869 by Leland Stanford, California's first Governor and founder of Stanford University.

The varietal wines produced are Pinot Chardonnay, Johannisberg Riesling, Pinot Noir, Cabernet Sauvignon, Gamay Beaujolais, Green Hungarian, Grey Riesling, Chenin Blanc, Zinfandel, and Grenache Rosé.

Appellation-of-origin and vintage-dated varietals are Chardonnay, North Coast and Santa Clara Valley; Johannisberg Riesling, North Coast; Pinot Noir, North Coast; Cabernet Sauvignon, North Coast; Gamay Beaujolais, North Coast; Pinot Noir Blanc, North Coast; Grey Riesling, North Coast; Chenin Blanc, North Coast; and Zinfandel, North Coast.

Generics are Chablis, Burgundy and Vin Rosé.

Mountain Wines are Mountain Chablis, Mountain Burgundy and Mountain Vin Rosé.

Proprietor's Special Reserve are Pinot Noir, Cabernet Sauvignon and Petite Sirah.

Sparkling Wines, Chardonnay Brut, Brut Champagne and Extra Dry Champagne.

Crackling Wines, Champagne Blanc de Blanc, Crackling Rosé, Crackling Duck, Muscato Spumante and Sparkling Green Hungarian.

Dessert Wines: Dry Bin Sherry, Classic Medium Sherry, Amber Cream Sherry, Rare Port, Cream of Black Muscat and Tangor.

Vermouths: Dry Vermouth and Sweet Vermouth.

Stanford Champagne.

The Winemaker's favorite is Green Hungarian and Estate-bottled Pinot Noir.

WENTE BROS.

5565 Tesla Road, Livermore, CA 94550
Alameda County

The Owner is the Wente Family. The Winemaker is William Joslin. Wente Bros. was founded in 1883 when Carl Wente planted the vineyard and built the winery in the Livermore Valley. Vineyards are at the winery and in the Arroyo Seco area of Monterey County.

100% varietal, vintage-dated wines produced are Gamay Beaujolais, Petite Sirah, Pinot Noir, Zinfandel, Blanc de Noir, Dry Semillon, Johannisberg Riesling, Pinot Blanc, Sauvignon Blanc and Chardonnay.

Also produced are Chablis, Rosé, Grey Riesling and Le Blanc de Blancs.

There are Wente Bros. Special Selections which are Arroyo Seco Riesling (100% Late Harvest White Riesling), and Gewurztraminer (100%).

The Winemaker's favorite wines are Pinot Chardonnay, Sauvignon Blanc, Petite Sirah, Johannisberg Riesling and Arroyo Sec Riesling.

MARK WEST VINEYARDS

7000 Trenton-Healdsburg Road, Forestville, CA 95436
Sonoma County

Owners are Robert and Joan Ellis. The Winemaker is

Aaron Mosley. Vineyard is located at the winery in the Russian River Valley. All wines are Estate-bottled with the exception of Zinfandel and French Colombard. They come from Geyserville selected vineyards.

The 100% varietal, vintage-dated, Estate-bottled wines produced are Chardonnay, Gewurztraminer, Johannisberg Riesling, Pinot Noir and Pinot Noir Blanc.

Also produced are 100% varietal, vintage-dated Zinfandel and French Colombard.

The Winemaker's favorite wine is the Chardonnay.

WHITEHALL LANE WINERY
1563 St. Helena, Hwy S., St. Helena CA 94574
Napa County

White Pinot (White Table Wine) (See Chenin Blanc)
White Riesling
(White Table Wine) (See Johannisberg Riesling)

White Table Wines
White dinner or table wines vary from extremely dry and tart to sweet and full-bodied. Their color ranges from pale straw to deep gold and their alcohol content from 10 to 14 percent. Most popular white dinner wines fall into three generic types: Chablis, Rhine or Sauterne. The varietal white wines are all discussed under their varietal name.

White Dinner Wines—Generic: Chablis, Moselle, Rhine, Sauterne, Vino Bianco.

White Table Wines—Varietal: Chardonnay (Pinot Chardonnay), Chenin Blanc, Emerald Riesling, French Colombard, Gewurztraminer, Pinot Blanc, Pinot Noir Blanc, Rkatsiteli, Sauvignon Blanc, Semillon, Sylvaner Riesling, Traminer, White Riesling (Johannisberg), Zinfandel Blanc.

DEAN WILLIAMS WINERY
1904 Pickett Rd., McKinleyville, CA
Humboldt County

WILLOW CREEK VINEYARD
1904 Pickett Road, McKinleyville, CA 95521
Lake County

Founded 1976. Owner is Dean Williams. Vineyards are located at the winery in the mountains.

Varietal, vintage-dated wines produced are Zinfandel, White Riesling, Pinot Noir, Grey Riesling, Gamay Beaujolais, Fumé Blanc, Chardonnay and Cabernet Sauvignon.

Also produced are Chenin Blanc, Burgundy and Chablis.

WILLOWSIDE VINEYARDS
1672 Willowside Rd., Santa Rosa, CA 95401
Sonoma County

Owner is the Beliz Family. The winemaker is Berle Beliz. Varietal, vintage-dated wines produced are Zinfandel, Pinot Noir, Pinot Chardonnay and Gewurztraminer. Vineyards, 24 acres in Sonoma County.

WINDSOR VINEYARDS
(See Sonoma Vineyards)

WINEMASTERS
(See Guild Wineries)

WINE AND THE PEOPLE
907 University Ave., Berkeley, CA 94710
Alameda County
Founded 1970. Founder and Winemaker is Peter R. Brehm. Not only a winery but also a home wine and beer supply house. Grapes purchased on a select vineyard basis.

Varietal, vintage-dated wines produced are a specialty Zinfandel Port, Dry Zinfandel and Cabernet Sauvignon. Also imports and deals in winemaking equipment and supplies for small wineries.

WINE BY WHEELER
(See Nicasio Vineyards)

WITTWER WINERY
2440 Frank Ave., Eureka, CA 95501
Humboldt County
Owner and Winemaker, J.R. Wittwer. Varietal wines produced are Cabernet Sauvignon and French Colombard.

WOODBRIDGE VINEYARD ASSN
4614 W. Turner Rd., Lodi, CA 95240
San Joaquin County
Founded 1905. Owner, Growers Cooperative; Winemaker, Jeffrey A. Moore. Primarily Bulk wines.

WOODBURY WINERY
32 Woodland Ave., San Rafael, CA
Marin County
Owner and Winemaker is Russell T. Woodbury. Grapes are purchased from Alexander Valley vineyards. Port wine is only wine produced.

Favorite wine of Winemaker is Vintage Port.

WOODSIDE VINEYARDS
340 Kings Mountain Road, Woodside, CA 94062
San Mateo County
Founded 1960. The Owners are Robert and Polly Mullen. The Winemaker is Mark Smith. Vineyards, 5 acres. The vineyard is located at the winery.

Varietal, vintage-dated wines produced are Cabernet Sauvignon, Pinot Noir and Chardonnay.

WOODEN VALLEY WINERY
Rt. 1, Box 124, Suisun, CA 94585
Solano County
Founded 1932. The Owners are Mario and Richard Lanza. Vineyards, 125 acres. The winery was founded in 1932.

Varietal wines produced are Riesling, Sauvignon Blanc, Zinfandel, Pinot Noir, Cabernet Sauvignon, Gamay Beaujolais and Carrignane.

Woody
The characteristic odor of "wet oak" is apparent in wine aged too long or in faulty wood. The term comes into use when this characteristic is excessive.

Y

YANKEE HILL WINERY
P.O. Box 163, Columbia, CA 95310
Tuolumne County
Founded 1974. The Owner and Winemaker is Ron Erickson.

Varietal, vintage-dated wines produced are Golden Bonanza Zinfandel and Columbia Cellars Zinfandel.

YERBA BUENA
Pier 33, San Francisco, CA 94111
President, Bryan R. R. Whipple; Vineyards, 22 acres in Sonoma County. Varietal wines produced are Pinot Noir (red, white, rose) and Gewurztraminer.

YOLO COUNTY
(Northern San Joaquin Valley) Harbor Winery, R & J Cook Winery

YORK MOUNTAIN WINERY
York Mt. Road, Templeton, CA 93465
San Luis Obispo County
The Owner is Max Goldman. The Winemaker is Steve Goldman. Founded by the York Family in 1882 and sold to Max Goldman in 1970. Max Goldman is former president of the American Society of Enologists. The vineyards are located at the winery in the Santa Lucia Mountains.

Varietal, vintage-dated wines produced are Zinfandel, Pinot Noir, Cabernet Sauvignon, Chardonnay, Merlot and Merlot Rosé.

Also produced is a Red wine (Barbera, Merlot-Ruby Cabernet Blend) and White wine (Chenin Blanc and Chardonnay Blend).

The Winemaker's favorite wine is Zinfandel.

YVERDON VINEYARDS
3787 Spring Mountain Road, Saint Helena, CA 94574
Napa County
Owner is Fred Aves. Vineyards are located at the winery site on Spring Mountain Road, a second in St. Helena and a third in the Napa Valley at the foot of Mt. St. Helena.

Varietal, vintage-dated wines produced are Cabernet Sauvignon, Gamay, Chenin Blanc, Johannisberg Riesling and Gewurztraminer.

Z

ZACA MESA WINERY
Foxen Canyon Road, Los Olivos, CA 93441
Santa Barbara County
Founded 1978. The President is Louis M. Ream. Winemaker is Ken Brown. Vineyards, 220 acres.

Varietal, vintage-dated Estate-bottled wines produced are Cabernet Sauvignon and Chardonnay.

ZAMPATTIS CELLAR
25445 Telarana Way, Carmel, CA 93923

Owner and Winemaker, Robert Zampatti.

ZD WINES

8383 Silverado Trail, Napa, CA 94558

Napa County

Founded 1969. Owners and Winemakers are Norman DeLuze and Gino Zepponi. Grapes are purchased on a select vineyard basis from Napa, Sonoma, Santa Barbara and San Luis Obispo Counties.

Varietal, vintage-dated wines produced are Chardonnay (100%), Pinot Noir (100%), Merlot (100%), Gewurztraminer (100%), Cabernet Sauvignon and Zinfandel. Also produced is Bacher Blanc (Sonoma).

Winemaker's favorite wines are Chardonnay and Pinot Noir.

Zin Blanca

(See Vose Vineyards)

Zinfandel

(Red Table Wine) A varietal grape that produces three styles of wine: Light—spicy flavor with a berry-like aroma and a tang. It should be consumed in one to three years. Serve with pastas and barbecues; Oak aged—intense, berry-like and spicy aroma, full-bodied with some tannin and dark in color. Should be aged 3 to 8 years. Serve with sausages, pastas and stews; Late Harvest—rich, dark, full-bodied, lots of alcohol and tannin. May be aged 8 to 16 years. Serve with Roquefort and rich game dishes. Look for the following: Alamaden, Ahern, Burgess, David Bruce, Caymus, Christian Bros, Callaway, Chateau Montelena, Cassayre-Forni, Carneros Creek, Cuvaison, Clos du Val, Dehlinger, Dry Creek, Fetzer, Gundlach Bundschu, Gemello, Hoffman Mountain Ranch, Kenwood, Lytton Springs, Robert Mondavi, Mirassou, Louis Martini, Mayacamas, J. W. Morris, Montevina, Masantuono, Joseph Phelps, Preston, J. Pedrocelli, Parducci, Rutherford Hill, Roudon-Smith, Ridge, Raymond, Sonoma, Simi, Sutter Home, Sebastiani.

Look for the following Zinfandel "Late Harvest": Cakebread, Cygnet Cellars, Dry Creek, Hacienda Wine Cellars, Monterey Peninsula, Monterey Vineyard (December Harvest), Mt. Veeder, Mount Eden, Montevina, Ridge.

Look for the following White Zinfandels: Richard Carey, Montevina, Baldinelli Vineyards, Vose Vineyards, Sutter Home.

California Vintage Chart

Unlike the wine growing regions of Europe, California has a relatively stable climate with consistent sunshine to ripen the grapes and produce reliable wine. However, there are some years that are truly outstanding in certain areas, particularly in the premium varietals. There are, of course, exceptions.

	North Coast (Napa, Sonoma, Mendocino)		Central Coast (Monterey, Santa Clara, etc.)	
	REDS	WHITES	REDS	WHITES
1968	★★★★	★★★★	★★★★	★★★★
1969	★★★	★★★	★★★	★★★
1970	★★★★	★★	★★★	★★★
1971	★★	★★	★	★
1972	★★	★	★	★
1973	★★★	★★	★★★	★★
1974	★★★★	★★★	★★★★	★★★
1975	★★★	★★★★	★★★	★★★
1976	★★★	★★★	★★★	★★★★
1977	★★★	★★★★	★★	★★★
1978	★★★★	★★★★	★★★★	★★★★
1979	too early	★★★	too early	★★★

★★★★ EXCEPTIONAL ★★★ VERY GOOD
★★ GOOD ★ FAIR

1980 Wine Ratings

Wine, like music and art is very subjective when it comes to personal taste. When it comes to judging the best, the sum total of a large panel of experts is the closest one can get when seeking an objective professional opinion. In my effort to be as objective as possible, it is my intention to bring you, the reader, the results of judgings by a group of California Winemakers. In this case, it is the Orange County Fair. Each year, I shall give you the total results of one or more such judging.

William I. Kaufman.

ORANGE COUNTY FAIR

1980 Wine Judging Awards.

Total wines judged: 733, including 11 varieties, 39 classifications. Judging Panel included 36 representatives of California Wineries, (a majority of whom were winemakers). All judging done on blind basis. Scoring done on University of California, Davis Modified 20 point system. Judging was done at South Coast Plaza Hotel, Costa Mesa, CA under auspices of the Orange County Fair and the Orange County Wine Society. All wines were purchased from retailers open to the public and *were not* specially submitted by the wineries.

LIST OF AWARD WINNERS

BLANC DE NOIR

49 Entries

(Low Price) (Under $4.00)

GOLD MEDALS: Trader Joe's NV Daybreak Blanc de Pinot Noir, Napa Valley.

SILVER MEDALS: Weibel 1979 Pinot Noir Blanc, Mendocino; Mill Creek 1979 Sonoma County Burgundy Blanc.

BRONZE MEDALS: Santa Ynez Valley 1979 Blanc de Cabernet Sauvignon.

(Medium Price) ($4.01 to $6.00)

No Gold Medals Awarded.

SILVER MEDALS: Grand Cru Vineyards 1979 Pinot Noir Blanc, Alexander Valley, Garden Creek Ranch; Johnson's Alexander Valley 1979 Pinot Noir Blanc.

BRONZE MEDALS: Hacienda Wine Cellars 1979

Pinot Noir Blanc, Sonoma County; Geyser Peak 1979 Sonoma County Pinot Noir Blanc; Kenwood 1979 Pinot Noir Blanc, Sonoma Valley; Franciscan 1978 Pinot Noir Blanc, Napa Valley.

(Premium Price) ($6.01 up)

No medals awarded.

CABERNET SAUVIGNON

143 Entries

(Low Price) (Under $5.00)

GOLD MEDALS: Bel Arbres NV California; Fetzer 1978 Lake County; Almaden 1977 Monterey; Fetzer 1977 Mendocino.

SILVER MEDALS: Barengo Vineyards 1976 Lake County; Christian Brothers NV Napa Valley.

BRONZE MEDALS: Franciscan 1976 Sonoma County; San Martin 1977 California; Raymond Hill 1976 Sonoma County (Trader Joe's): Giumarra NV California; R.J. Cook 1978 Red Table Wine, Clarksburg (made entirely from Cabernet Sauvignon grapes)

(Medium Price) ($5.01 to $10.00)

GOLD MEDALS: Trefethen Vineyards 1976 Napa Valley; Sebastiani NV No. California; Rutherford Hill 1976 Napa Valley; Caymus Vineyards 1976 Napa Valley Estate Bottled; Lower Lake 1977 Lake County, Stromberg's Hummel Lane Vineyard; Raymond 1977 Napa Valley, Estate Bottled; Freemark Abbey 1975 Napa Valley; Monterey Peninsula Winery 1977 Monterey; Boeger 1977 El Dorado County.

SILVER MEDALS: Dehlinger Winery 1977 Sonoma County; Beaulieu Vineyard 1977 Rutherford, Estate Bottled; Diamond Creek 1977 Red Rock Terrace, First Pick; Estrella River Winery 1977 San Luis Obispo, Estate Bottled; Grand Cru Vineyards NV Alexander Valley, Garden Creek Ranch (Lot CS 767); Diamond Creek 1977 Gravelly Meadow; Souverain 1976 No. Coast; Richard Carey Winery 1975 Lake County (Cask 714),: Sterling Vineyards 1976 Napa Valley, Estate Bottled.

BRONZE MEDALS: Stag's Leap Wine Cellars 1977 Napa Valley; Rancho Yerba Buena 1978 Alexander Valley; Field Stone 1977 Alexander Valley, Estate Bottled; Hacienda Wine Cellars 1977 Sonoma Valley; Chateau Montelena 1975 No. Coast; Harbor Winery 1977 Amador County, Deaver Vineyards; Beringer 1976 Sonoma Knight's Valley Estate; Sebastiani 1973 Proprietor's Reserve; Robert Mondavi 1977 Napa Valley; Callaway 1977 Temecula, Estate Bottled; Sommelier Winery 1977 San Luis Obispo; Mario Perelli-Minetti 1977 Napa Valley; Lambert Bridge 1976 Sonoma County; Parducci 1977 Mendocino County; HMR Vineyards 1976 Paso Robles, Estate Bottled; Chateau Chevalier 1978 Napa Valley; Clos Du Val 1977 Napa Valley; Rutherford Vintners 1977 Napa Valley.

(Premium Price) ($10.01 up)

GOLD MEDALS: Ridge 1976 York Creek; Heitz Cellars 1975 Martha's Vineyard.

SILVER MEDALS: Conn Creek 1976 Napa; Villa Mt.

Eden 1977 Napa; Buena Vista 1974 Sonoma (Cask 25); Joseph Phelps 1977 Napa.

BRONZE MEDALS: Charles Krug 1974 Napa Lot F-1 Vintage Select.

CHARDONNAY

99 Entries

(Low Price) (Under $6.00)

GOLD MEDALS: Louis M. Martini 1978 California Pinot Chardonnay; Sonoma Vineyards 1978 Sonoma County; River Oaks Vineyard 1978 Alexander Valley.

SILVER MEDALS: Parducci 1979 Mendocino County.

BRONZE MEDALS: Paul Masson 1978 Monterey County, Estate Bottled; Geyser Peak 1978 Sonoma County.

(Medium Price) ($6.01 to $11.00)

GOLD MEDALS: Trefethen 1977 Napa Valley; Chateau St. Jean 1979 Sonoma; Zaca Mesa 1978 Santa Ynez Valley, Barrel Fermented; Estrella River Winery 1978 San Luis Obispo; Navarro 1978 Mendocino; Smothers 1979 California.

SILVER MEDALS: Landmark 1978 Sonoma County; Zaca Mesa 1978 Santa Ynez Valley; Alexander Valley Vineyards 1978 Alexander Valley; Chateau Montelena 1978 California; The Firestone Vineyard 1978 Santa Ynez Valley; Sonoma Vineyards 1978 River West Vineyard, Estate Bottled; Rutherford Hill 1978 Napa Valley; HMR Vineyards 1978 San Luis Obispo.

BRONZE MEDALS: Dry Creek Vineyard 1978 Sonoma County; Cuvaison 1977 Napa Valley; Parducci 1979 Cellar Master's, Mendocino County; Jekel Vineyards 1978 Monterey County; Stonegate 1978 No. Coast; Buena Vista 1978 Sonoma Pinot Chardonnay; Conn Creek 1978 Napa Valley; HMR Vineyards 1977 Paso Robles, Estate Bottled; Pendleton 1978 Monterey; Carneros Creek 1978 Sonoma County; Franciscan 1978 Temecula; Burgess 1978 Napa Valley; Clos du Bois 1978 2nd Release, Alexander Valley.

(Premium Price) ($11.01 up)

GOLD MEDALS: Chateau St. Jean 1978 Robert Young Vineyards; Grgich Hills Cellar 1977 Napa Valley.

SILVER MEDALS: Robert Mondavi 1978 Napa Valley; Villa Mt. Eden 1978 Napa Valley.

No Bronze Medals Awarded.

CHENIN BLANC DRY

19 Entries

No entries in Low Price Class

(Medium Price) ($3.51 to $5.00)

GOLD MEDALS: Stevenot Winery 1979 No. California; McDowell Valley Vineyards 1979 Mendocino County, Estate Bottled.

SILVER MEDALS: Callaway 1979 Temecula, Estate Bottled.

BRONZE MEDALS: Louis J. Foppiano 1979 No. California; Pope Valley 1979 Napa County.

(Premium Price) ($5.01 up)

No Medals Awarded

CHENIN BLANC SWEET

67 Entries

(Low Price) (Under $3.50)

GOLD MEDALS: Giumarra NV California; Trader Joe's 1979 California.

SILVER MEDALS: Pedroncelli 1979 Sonoma County.

BRONZE MEDALS: Richard Carey Winery NV California (Lot 781); Taylor California Cellars NV California; Inglenook NV "Navalle" California.

(Medium Price) ($3.51 to $5.00)

GOLD MEDALS: Charles Krug NV Napa Valley; Beringer 1979 Napa Valley; HMR Vineyards 1979 Central Coast Counties, Demi-Sec.

SILVER MEDALS: San Pasqual Vineyards 1979 San Diego County, Estate Bottled; Parducci 1979 Mendocino County; San Martin 1978 California; Lawrence Winery NV California.

BRONZE MEDALS: Paul Masson NV California; Congress Springs 1979 Santa Cruz Mountains Vineyard, St. Charles; Alamaden 1978 Monterey; The Monterey Vineyard 1978 Monterey County; J. Lohr 1979 No. California; Yverdon 1978 Napa Valley.

(Premium price) ($5.01 up)

GOLD MEDALS: Robert Mondavi 1979 Napa Valley.

SILVER MEDALS: Simi Winery 1978 Mendocino County; Stag's Leap Vintners 1979 Napa Valley.

BRONZE MEDALS: Mt. Veeder Winery 1979 Napa County, Bernstein Vineyard.

DRY SHERRY

27 Entries

(Low Price) (Under $3.00)

GOLD MEDALS: Assumption Abbey Sherry Palido Pale Dry.

SILVER MEDALS: Almaden California Solera Flor Fino.

BRONZE MEDALS: Concannon Prelude; Paul Masson Cocktail; Gallo Old Decanter Brand, Very Dry; Charles Krug Pale Dry; Inglenook Pale Dry.

(Medium Price) ($3.01 to $4.50)

No Gold Medals Awarded

SILVER MEDALS: Weibel Solera Flor Dry Bin.

BRONZE MEDALS: Louis M. Martini Dry; Setrakian Solera Dry.

(Premium Price) ($4.51 up)

GOLD MEDALS: Angelo Papagni Finest Hour Dry.

SILVER MEDALS: Sebastiani Arenas Dry.

No Bronze Medals Awarded

GEWURZTRAMINER

52 Entries

(Low Price) (Under $4.50)

No Gold Medals Awarded.

No Silver Medals Awarded.

BRONZE MEDALS: San Martin 1978 Santa Barbara County.

(Medium Price) ($4.51 to $7.00)

GOLD MEDALS: Parducci 1979 Mendocino County.

SILVER MEDALS: Grand Cru Vineyards 1979 Alexander Valley, Garden Creek Ranch; Wente Bros. 1978 Monterey, Arroyo Seco Vineyard; Buena Vista 1978 Sonoma; Souverain 1978 No. Coast; Kenwood 1979 Sonoma Valley.

BRONZE MEDALS: Felton Empire California 1979 Maritime Vineyard Series Dry; The Monterey Vineyard 1978 Monterey County.

(Premium Price) ($7.01 up)

GOLD MEDALS: Smothers 1979 Alexander Valley, Late Harvest; Felton Empire 1979 Santa Barbara, Tepesquet Vineyard.

SILVER MEDALS: Chateau St. Jean 1979 Belle Terre & Robert Young Vineyards.

BRONZE MEDALS: Richard Carey Winery 1979 Late Harvest, Santa Barbara County.

PETITE SIRAH
46 Entries

(Low Price) (Under $4.50)

GOLD MEDALS: Louis J. Foppiano 1976 Russian River Valley; Fortino Winery 1977 California.

SILVER MEDALS: Giumarra NV California; Inglenook 1975 Napa Valley, Estate Bottled; Wente Bros. 1977 California.

BRONZE MEDALS: Bel Arbres 1977 Mendocino.

(Medium Price) ($4.51 to $6.50)

GOLD MEDALS: Souverain 1976 No. Coast.

SILVER MEDALS: Round Hill Vineyards 1977 Napa Valley; Sonoma Vineyards 1975 No. California; Stag's Leap Vineyard 1976 Napa Valley.

BRONZE MEDALS: Rosenblum Cellars 1978 Napa.

(Premium Price) ($6.51 up)

No Gold Medals Awarded

SILVER MEDALS: Burgess 1977 Napa Valley; Field Stone 1977 Alexander Valley.

BRONZE MEDALS: Hop Kiln 1977 Russian River Valley.

SAUVIGNON BLANC
50 Entries

(Low Price) (Under $4.50)

No Gold Medals Awarded

SILVER MEDALS: San Martin 1978 California (Fumé Blanc); Parducci 1979 Mendocino County.

BRONZE MEDALS: Bel Arbras 1977 Napa (Fumé Blanc)

(Medium Price) ($4.51 to $7.00)

GOLD MEDALS: Franciscan 1979 California (Fumé Blanc); Santa Ynez Valley Winery 1979 California.

SILVER MEDALS: Chateau St. Jean 1979 Sonoma County (Fumé Blanc); Louis J. Foppiano 1978 Sonoma (Fumé Blanc).

BRONZE MEDALS: Davis Bynum Winery 1978 Sonoma (Fumé Blanc), Rochioli-Harrison Reserve; Dry Creek Vineyard 1979 Sonoma County (Fumé Blanc); Buena Vista 1978 Mendocino; Fetzer 1979 Mendocino (Fumé Blanc)

(Premium Price) ($7.01 up)

GOLD MEDALS: Robert Mondavi 1978 Napa Valley (Fumé Blanc)

No Silver Medals Awarded.

BRONZE MEDALS: Veedercrest 1979 Sonoma County, Shiloh Vineyard.

PINOT NOIR

67 Entries.

(Low Price) (Under $5.00)

GOLD MEDALS: Clos du Bois 1977 Sonoma County, Dry Creek.

SILVER MEDALS: Weibel 1975 No. Coast

BRONZE MEDALS: Sebastiani NV No. California; Cresta Blanca 1975 California; Round Hill Vineyards 1976 No. Coast.

(Medium Price) ($5.01 to $7.50)

GOLD MEDALS: Pendleton 1978 Monterey; Beringer 1975 Mendocino.

SILVER MEDALS: Inglenook 1973 Napa Valley (Cask B-7), Estate Bottled; Gundlach-Bundschu 1977 Sonoma Valley; Martin Ray NV La Montana, Cuvee 3; Sonoma Vineyards 1976 River East Vineyard, Estate Bottled; Trefethen 1976 Napa Valley; Robert Mondavi 1977 Napa Valley.

BRONZE MEDALS: Parducci 1976 Cellar Master's, Mendocino County; Caymus 1976 Napa Valley; Rutherford Hill 1976 Napa Valley.

(Premium Price) ($7.51 up)

GOLD MEDALS: Kenwood 1977 Sonoma Valley, Jack London.

SILVER MEDALS: Beaulieu Vineyards 1976 Los Carneros, Napa Valley; Veedercrest 1978 Sonoma County.

BRONZE MEDALS: HMR Vineyards 1976 Paso Robles, Estate Bottled.

ZINFANDEL

109 Entries.

(Low Price) (Under $3.50)

GOLD MEDALS: Fetzer 1977 Lolonis, Mendocino (*); Parducci 1978 Mendocino County.

(*)This wine inadvertently judged in incorrect price classification.

SILVER MEDALS: Berkeley Wine Cellars 1977 Kelley Creek, Sonoma County (Wine & The People); Bel Arbres 1975 Sonoma.

BRONZE MEDALS: Wente Bros. 1978 California; Giumarra NV California; River Oaks Vineyard 1977 Alexander Valley; Fetzer 1978 Lake County.

(Medium Price) ($3.51 to $5.50)

GOLD MEDALS: Sierra Vista 1978 El Dorado County; Preston 1977 Sonoma County, Dry Creek Valley; Zaca Mesa 1977 Santa Ynez Valley.

SILVER MEDALS: Smothers 1978 San Luis Obispo; Montevina 1978 Amador County; Estrella River Winery 1977 San Luis Obispo; Harbor Winery 1977 Shenandoah Valley, Deaver Vineyard; Ridge 1977 San Luis III; Kenwood 1977 Sonoma County.

BRONZE MEDALS: Lawrence Winery 1979 California; Dry Creek Vineyard 1977 Sonoma County; Parducci

1978 Cellar Master's Mendocino County; Boeger Winery 1978 El Dorado County; Callaway 1977 Temecula, Estate Bottled; Louis M. Martini 1976 California; Napa Wine Cellar 1978 Alexander Valley.

(Premium Price) ($5.51 up)

GOLD MEDALS: Mastantuono 1978 Templeton, San Luis Obispo, Dusi Vineyard; Gundlach-Bundschu 1977 Sonoma Valley, Rhine Farm Vineyards, Estate Bottled; Clos du Val 1977 Napa Valley; Joseph Phelps 1977 Alexander Valley, Black Mountain Vineyard; Milano 1978 Mendocino County, Redwood Valley, Garzini Vineyards.

SILVER MEDALS: Chateau Montelena 1976 No. Coast; Cassayre-Forni 1977 Sonoma County; Stony Ridge 1977 Livermore Valley, Reutz Vineyard; Sommelier 1977 Lodi Lot II; HMR Vineyards 1976 Sauret Vineyards, San Luis Obispo.

BRONZE MEDALS: Lytton Springs 1978 Sonoma County; Hop Kiln 1978 Russian River Valley; Cuvaison 1976 Napa Valley; Davis Bynum Winery 1977 Sonoma; Ridge 1978 Shenandoah, Esola Vineyard.

ZINFANDEL LATE HARVEST DRY & SWEET

5 Entries

No entries low price dry

(Medium Price Dry) ($5.01 to $7.50)

SILVER MEDALS: Grand Cru Vineyards 1977 Sonoma Late Picked, Estate Bottled.

(Premium Price Dry) ($7.51 up)

GOLD MEDALS: Mt. Veeder 1978 Napa County.

BRONZE MEDALS: Ridge 1977 Geyserville, Trentadue Ranch.

No entries low price sweet.

No awards medium price sweet.

(Premium Price Sweet) ($10.01 up)

SILVER MEDALS: Johnson's Alexander Valley 1978 Alexander Valley, Lot 1, Estate Bottled.

JUDGES ORANGE COUNTY FAIR COMMERCIAL WINE JUDGING—1980

Jim Ahern, Ahern Winery
Richard Arrowood, Chateau St. Jean
Dave Bennion, Ridge Vineyards
Ken Brown, Zaca Mesa Winery
Jim Carter, Sebastiani Vineyards
Charles Crawford, Gallo Winery
Al Cribari, Cribari & Sons
Richard Elwood, Llords & Elwood
John Hoffman, Christian Brothers
Bill Jekel, Jekel Vineyards
John Kenworthy, Kenworthy Vineyards
George Kolarovich, Perelli-Minetti
Robert Kozlowski, Kenwood Vineyards
Ray Krause, California House Wine Co
Jim Lawrence, Lawrence Winery
Zelma Long, Simi Winery/Long Vineyards
John Merritt, Gundlach-Bundschu Winery
Bonny Meyer, Silver Oak Cellars
(continued)

Steve Mirassou, Mirassou Vineyards
Tim Mondavi, Robert Mondavi Winery
Myron Nightingale, Beringer Vineyards
Steve O'Donnell, Callaway Vineyards
Angelo Papagni, Papagni Vineyards
John Parducci, Parducci Winery
Ed Pedrizzetti, Pedrizzetti Winery
Phyllis Pedrizzetti, Pedrizzetti Winery
Jim Prager, Prager Wine & Port Works
Mike Rowan, Jordan Winery
Dawnine Sample, Domaine Chandon
Leon Sobon, Shenandoah Vineyards
David Stare, Dry Creek Vineyards
Peter Stern, Turgeon-Lohr Winery
Rodney Strong, Sonoma Vineyards
Nils Venge, Villa Mt. Eden Winery
Warren Winiarski, Stag's Leap Wine Cellars
Frank Woods, Clos Du Bois

About the Author

THE POCKET ENCYCLOPEDIA OF CALIFORNIA WINE is William I. Kaufman's 134th published book. Writer, lecturer, photographer, song writer, television spokesman and creator of television ideas, he has covered the fields of food, wine, entertaining and travel. His most recent wine books have been *The Whole World Catalog of Wine* and *The Travelers Guide to the Vineyards of North America.* One of the most beautiful wine books ever created was *Champagne* which he wrote and illustrated. *Perfume* is another example of his magnificent photography. His books have been translated into many languages. Mr. Kaufman is recipient of many foreign honors including the Chevalier de l'Ordre du Merite Agricole from the French Republic. He received the Christopher Award for his UNICEF childrens books songs, poems, prayers and legends. He has had twenty major photographic exhibitions including two major color exhibitions by Kodak. His publishers include: Doubleday, Harper & Row, Penguin, Viking, Dell, Simon & Shuster. He is a member of the Southern California Wine Writers, and is active on wine tasting and judging panels.